William Nicholas

Christianity and Socialism

William Nicholas

Christianity and Socialism

ISBN/EAN: 9783742867865

Manufactured in Europe, USA, Canada, Australia, Japa

Cover: Foto ©Thomas Meinert / pixelio.de

Manufactured and distributed by brebook publishing software
(www.brebook.com)

William Nicholas

Christianity and Socialism

CHRISTIANITY

AND

SOCIALISM.

THE TWENTY-THIRD FERNLEY LECTURE.

DELIVERED IN CARDIFF, JULY 28, 1893.

BY THE

REV. WILLIAM NICHOLAS, M.A., D.D.

London:

WESLEYAN METHODIST BOOK ROOM,
2, CASTLE STREET, CITY ROAD, E.C.;
AND 66, PATERNOSTER ROW, E.C.

1893

CONTENTS.

v

CHAPTER XVII.

Present Condition of Society unsatisfactory—Hopeful Tendencies in Society—Evils of Socialism—Impossibility of establishing Socialism—Sufficiency of Christianity .   .   .   .   *pp.* 215–218

INDEX OF SUBJECTS AND PERSONS .   *pp.* 219, 220

LIST OF AUTHORS QUOTED OR REFERRED TO.

ATKINSON'S *Distribution of Profits.*
BAX'S (BELFORT) *Religion of Socialism ; Ethics of Socialism.*
BEAULIEU'S (LEROY) *Papacy, Socialism, and Democracy.*
BOOTH'S (CHARLES) *Pauperism.*
BRACE'S *Gesta Christi.*
COOK'S (J.) *Socialism ; Labour.*
DAWSON'S *State Socialism and Prince Bismarck ; German Socialism and Ferdinand Lassalle ; The Unearned Increment.*
Fabian Essays.
FARRAR'S *Social Questions.*
GEORGE'S (HENRY) *Progress and Poverty ; Social Problems.*
GIFFEN'S (Dr.) *The Progress of the Working Classes.*
GRAHAM'S *Socialism New and Old.*
INGRAM'S *History of Political Economy.*
KIRKUP'S *History of Socialism.*
LEO XIII.'s *Encyclical, "De Conditione Opificum."*
M'CULLOCH'S *Principles of Political Economy.*
MALLET'S (Sir F.) *Free Exchange.*
MARX'S *Das Kapital.*
MILL'S (J. S.) *Liberty ; Representative Government ; Principles of Political Economy.*
MITCHELL'S *The Drink Question.*
RAE'S *Contemporary Socialism.*
RITCHIE'S *Principles of State Interference.*
ROGERS' (THOROLD) *Work and Wages.*
RYLANCE'S *Social Questions.*
SCHAEFFLE'S *The Quintessence of Socialism.*
SMITH'S (ADAM) *Wealth of Nations.*
SPENCER'S (HERBERT) *Man versus The State ; Social Statics ; Sociology.*

CHRISTIANITY AND SOCIALISM.

CHAPTER I.

Social Nature of Man—Evils of Society—Jesus of Nazareth a Social
Reformer—Socialism and Christianity—Historical Development
of Socialism—The French Revolution—Carlyle—Joseph Babœuf
—Spread of Socialism—Social Condition of Germany—Prince
Bismarck.

GOD has made man a social being. In his earliest years
his very existence depends upon the watchfulness and care
and kindness of others. As he grows up society is necessary for the development of his faculties. Ideas are
imparted to him by the conversation of those by whom
he is surrounded, and his emotions are stirred by their
conduct. He imitates, or emulates, or disdains their
example. By the writings of others, distant from him in
space or in time, or in both, other ideas are imparted and
other emotions are stirred ; and these influences acting on
his original disposition, by sympathy or by antagonism, his
nature is developed, his opinions are formed, and his
character determined.

Man has in him a gregarious instinct, so that society is
necessary to his happiness.

> Oh for a lodge in some vast wilderness,
> Some boundless contiguity of shade !

I

expresses a morbid, not a normal condition. The sound mind in a sound body desires to mingle with men and to act its part in the great drama of human life.

Society is not to be regarded as a mere accumulation of separate and distinct individuals coming into contact with each other, as grains of sand on the ocean shore, without having any vital bond of union between them. It is rather to be regarded as an organism, past, present, and future vitally connected together, all influencing each and each influencing all. As in the body, if one member suffers all the members suffer with it, if one member rejoices all rejoice with it, if one member—say the brain or the heart —does not fulfil its function, the whole body is injured ; so in society, those who do wrong or who fail in doing their duty injure the whole, and those who do right, who faith-fully perform their allotted task, benefit the whole. The welfare, or the reverse, of society is thus determined by the character and conduct of the individuals who compose it, as the condition of any aggregate will be determined by that of its component parts.

The condition of society will then just vary as the characters of the units that compose it varies. When men individually are selfish and licentious, false and full of greed, heedless of their duty to God and the rights of their fellows ; when men are " like a vase of Egyptian asps, each one trying to get its head above the others " : then there will be oppression and discontent, unlawful gains and poverty, honest and dishonest, squalor in rags and luxury in purple, envy on the one hand and pride on the other, mutual distrust and mutual hatred. This condition may become so aggravated that a revolution is the inevitable result, or it may be so modified by the number of honest, unselfish, brotherly men—who are " the salt of the earth " —that society is preserved from dissolution, and normal development ensues.

At various periods in the history of the world, when the state of society has been well-nigh intolerable, men with a strong sense of justice, a hatred of oppression, deep sympathy with the suffering masses, or motives not so creditable, have stood forth as social reformers. Not always have social reformers been wise in their generation. It is true that often they have very clearly and indeed powerfully pointed out the existing evils; yet their proposals have been sometimes utopian and impracticable, and sometimes plausible but injurious, inasmuch as whilst removing some evils they would introduce other and worse ones. Then we have had social reformers who spoke the words of truth and soberness, and whose remedies were potent to purge the body politic of its malady and bring it to perfect soundness.

At the head of all social reformers we place Jesus of Nazareth. The period of His birth was one of exceptional darkness. " Darkness covered the earth, and gross darkness the peoples." Ever since the Dayspring from on high visited us has the day been growing brighter.

When Christ was born, in the Roman world it was an age of unbelief. Julius Cæsar, the chief pontiff of Rome, in his speech against Catiline, objected to his being put to death, on the ground that "death is a rest from troubles to those in grief and misery, not a punishment; it ends all the evils of life, for there is neither care nor joy beyond it." Here we have an official and deliberate denial of the immor-

tality of the soul.   Men had ceased to have any real belief
in the gods.   " To the multitude all religions were equally
true, to the magistrate all equally useful, and to the philosopher all equally false."   Unbridled lust and cruelty prevailed.   Prisoners were tortured.   Tens of thousands of
men were held in slavery ; and whilst the man who killed
a ploughing ox was punished, he who killed a slave of his
own was called to no account whatever.   Beggars herded
together in crowds, and on their appeals for charity were
repelled with scorn.   No one of all the rich men living in
luxurious Roman villas ever founded an asylum for the
poor or a hospital for the sick.   Morals were so depraved,
that noble Roman matrons, in order to avoid the penalties
for adultery, enrolled themselves on the lists of public
prostitutes.

In Judæa, the Holy Land, relentless faction, gross licentiousness, unscrupulous avarice, heartless neglect and oppression of the poor, with the added evil of hypocrisy, marked
the degenerate sons of Abraham, who boasted of him as
their father, but whose sublime and simple faith they did
not inherit.

Into this world of unbelief and immorality, of cruelty
and wretchedness, Jesus came.   He came as a great theological teacher, telling men of God, and of the eternal future,
and of duty.   He came to give men an example of holy
living, to present His abstract doctrine of duty in concrete
form.   He came, in order that by His sacrificial death He
might make " a full, perfect, and sufficient sacrifice, oblation,
and satisfaction for the sins of the whole world."   But He
came in addition as a great social reformer.

The common people heard Him gladly.   Why ?   Not

altogether because they were attracted and impressed by His miracles, not altogether because His earnest and straightforward teaching appealed to their nature, less conventional than that of the ruling classes or the priestly caste, not altogether because they were dissatisfied with their condition and eager for novelty, but because they felt that He was their friend, that amidst neglect—as sheep without a shepherd—He was on their side and took their part.

And they were right. He was the friend of the poor, and the afflicted, and the downtrodden, and the outcast. He condemns the sins of those who had wealth and power. "Woe unto you, scribes and Pharisees, hypocrites! for ye devour widows' houses, and for a pretence make long prayers: therefore ye shall receive the greater damnation. . . . Woe unto you, scribes and Pharisees, hypocrites! for ye pay tithe of mint and anise and cummin, and have omitted the weightier matters of the law, judgment, mercy, and faith: these ought ye to have done, and not to leave the other undone. . . . Woe unto you, scribes and Pharisees, hypocrites! for ye make clean the outside of the cup and of the platter, but within they are full of extortion and excess. . . . Woe unto you, scribes and Pharisees, hypocrites! for ye are like unto whited sepulchres, which indeed appear beautiful outward, but are within full of dead men's bones, and of all uncleanness."

No wonder the common people heard gladly one who could thus speak, and with no "bated breath and whispering humbleness" could thus speak out against the evildoers and frauds and oppressors of His day. Jesus of Nazareth is the greatest of social reformers, and the system

He taught, if cast into the bitter well of our humanity, will make the waters sweet. Christianity—and by that word we understand the system of faith and morals taught by Jesus and His apostles, and contained in the New Testament—Christianity when regarded, not merely as a theory or a sentiment, as a something to discuss or to admire, but received by a living faith and made by that faith an operating power in the entire life, is capable of healing the deadly plague of society, and of enabling men to live a fully developed, well rounded, and joyous life, even in this world of sin and death.

Now there is another system which claims to have a deep sympathy with the poor and the suffering, and declares itself able to remove all social evils, and to solve all social problems, and to so reconstruct society that men shall lead lives free from the cares and troubles of the present, and with full satisfaction to themselves. This system is Socialism, and we are to consider it particularly in its relation to Christianity.

These two systems are gravely dissimilar in origin, in principles, in aims, in methods, and in motives.

It is true that there is some ground common to both. To a certain extent they overlap. That Socialist writers and leaders have consciously or unconsciously derived sentiments and ideas from Christianity is certain. Yet, because of this common ground, to represent the two systems as similar, or as allied, or as closely related to each other, is a mistake. We have been told that every Christian is a bit of a Socialist, and that every Socialist is a bit of a Christian. Now, would any one say that because there is some ground common to Christianity and to

Mohammedanism, therefore every Christian is a bit of a Mohammedan, and every Mohammedan is a bit of a Christian ?

Sometimes the difference between the two systems is minified in order that Socialists may be gained to Christianity. To try to make a convert of a Socialist by telling him that there is but little difference between Socialism and Christianity, is not compatible with "simplicity and godly sincerity," and may only lead to disappointment and increased antagonism, when Christianity is more fully known and the artifice discovered. No one likes to be caught with guile. Here as elsewhere "honesty is the best policy."

On the other hand, for a Christian who may be an earnest philanthropist and impatient of surrounding evils, who is not perhaps sufficiently considerate of the perplexity of life, who would like to see less inequality in the distribution of wealth, hastily to call himself a Socialist, may bring him into very strange company, and lead him to feel, when he discovers the principles and practices of his new associates, that he has made a mistake and must retrace his steps, or become the subject of perpetual misunderstandings, or else—worst of all!—he may gradually lose his hold of Christianity, and let the worse creed cast out the better.

Deep pity, earnest desire, and practical effort for the amelioration of the hard lot of the poor man, with his dependent family, out of employ, or of the poor man struggling on under a heavy burden, and receiving what are called, and sometimes rightly called, "starvation wages," may be experienced by those who are not, as well as by those who are, Socialists. The theories of Herbert

Spencer and of the Socialists are at opposite poles, yet he
writes sympathetically and well :

" The fates of the great majority have ever been, and
doubtless still are, so sad that it is painful to think of
them. Unquestionably the existing type of social organization is one which none who cares for their kind can
contemplate with satisfaction ; and unquestionably men's
activities accompanying this type are far from being
admirable. The strong divisions of rank and the immense
inequalities of means are at variance with that ideal of
human relations on which the sympathetic imagination
likes to dwell ; and the average conduct under the pressure
and excitement of social life, as at present carried on, is in
sundry respects repulsive."

There are a large number of men who believe that many
things under the present *régime* are unjust and ought to be
changed, that laws should wisely promote the diffusion of
wealth and not its extreme concentration, that the active
business and not the idle interest should be favoured, that
as in the family the weak one is taken special care of, so
in the State those who are unable to take care of themselves ought to be efficiently protected. There are many
who believe that labour ought to get its full reward, that
men by associating themselves together should help one
another and accomplish by co-operation what they could
never accomplish without it, that the State may be rightly
called upon to help society by doing whatever can be done
better by State organization than by private enterprise.
Yet these men are not Socialists, and distinctly repudiate
the name as well as the principles and methods of Socialism.
As the author of *Papacy, Democracy, and Socialism* says :

" It is right that words should preserve the sense which
usage has given them, not only to enable us to understand
one another when we speak, but also because it is not right
that the defenders and the enemies of home and property
should assume the same name, and should, even apparently,
adopt the same colours, or march under the same flag.   It
is not possible to disarm revolutionary passions and refute
submissive doctrines by borrowing their vocabulary ; on the
contrary, if you take the name, you may often be compelled
to submit to the thing."

We want then to answer, with as much accuracy as
possible, the following questions : What is Socialism ? what
are the principles that dominate it ? what are the objects
at which it aims ? what are the methods that it is ready
to use ? what are the motives by which it is inspired ?

Now, in order to do this, we must trace the historical
development of Socialism, and in doing so we shall endeavour to let leading Socialists express their own opinions
in their own language regarding this, as a much fairer
method than that of paraphrasing their opinions ; for nothing
is easier, even with every wish to be fair, than to misrepresent an opponent.

Socialists tells us that Socialism is the last word of the
Revolution of 1789, and that the movement then begun
must sooner or later end in a democratic communism.
Before the French Revolution, oppression, which makes a
wise man mad, had reached a point at which it was no
longer endurable.   Life was not worth living—so far as
the masses were concerned.   The few revelled in luxury,
in licentiousness, in wanton cruelty and insolence.   The
many toiled hard, and had a meagre subsistence.   Neither

their humanity nor their citizenship was respected. Law permitted a seigneur, as he returned from hunting, to kill not more than two serfs, that he might refresh his feet in their warm blood. A keen sportsman amuses himself by shooting down plumbers and slaters, and sees them roll from their roofs with more gratification than if he had brought down an equal number of partridges or grouse.

Then these superiors, cruel, wanton, luxurious, were in general devoid of qualities calculated to gain the affection, the confidence, the admiration, or even the fear of the populace.

The masses, treated as beings who had duties but had no rights, who were the despised instruments of their superiors' greed, or ambition, or pleasure, conceived, as might be expected, a burning and bitter class hatred. They rose in rebellion, and, returning ferocity for ferocity and scorn for scorn, overturned the then existing social order. King and queen, nobles, clergy, and gentry, as well as many of the *bourgeoisie*, perished in the " Terror."

In what is probably his best work, Carlyle, speaking of the forces that caused this Revolution, says: " Powerfulest of all, least recognised of all, a Noblesse of Literature ; without steel on their thigh, without gold in their purse, but with the ' grand thaumaturgic faculty of Thought ' in their head. French Philosophism has arisen ; in which little word how much do we include ! Here, indeed, lies properly the cardinal symptom of the whole widespread malady. Faith is gone out; Scepticism is come in."

Modern Socialism was generated out of the notions about property, and the State, and the origin and objects of civil society maintained by these philosophers. They are proclaimed about the same period by many able writers : by Brissot, by Malby, by Morelly, and above all by Rousseau. Their leading thought was to restore what they called the state of nature, when primitive equality still reigned, and the earth belonged to none, but the fruits of it to all, when there was common possession and common enjoyment. They taught that there was no foundation for property but need. He who needed a thing had a right to it, and he who had more than he needed was a thief. Rousseau said every man had naturally a right to whatever he needed ; and Brissot, anticipating the famous words of Proudhon, declared that in a state of nature " exclusive property was theft." It was so in a state of nature, but it was so also in a state of society ; for society was built on a social contract, " the clauses of which reduce themselves to one, *viz.* the total transfer of each associate, with all his rights, to the community." This makes the individual nothing, it makes the State everything. Property is only so much of the national estate, conditionally conceded to the individual. He has the right to use it because the State permits him, while the State permits him, and how the State permits him. So with every other right ; he is to think, speak, train his children as the State directs and allows, in the interest of the common good. Thus objecting to one slavery, they seek another and a worse one, and entirely forget that the object of society ought to be to *protect* natural rights, and not to *destroy* them.

These ideas remained as nebulous hypotheses till they were systematised by Joseph Babœuf. He edited a journal at Amiens, and ardently supported the Revolution, was twice tried on account of the violence of his writing, but was acquitted. He joined a secret society, whose plans were divulged by one of the members, and was condemned for conspiracy to be guillotined. On hearing the sentence he stabbed himself, but was borne bleeding and dying to the scaffold in May, 1797. Such was the end of the man who may most justly be called the father of modern Socialism.

Some four years before this tragedy, in 1793, Babœuf discarded his Christian name of Joseph, because, as he said, he did not desire the virtues of Joseph, took the name of Caius Gracchus, and organized the conspiracy of the Egaux. Then modern Socialism began. He conducted an incendiary journal called *The Tribune of the People*, and in it promulgated his views. His desire was to form a true democratic republic, which was to be brought about by the diffusion of his views in his paper, and chiefly by the action of his secret society. At the appointed time the patriots were to muster, with banners flying, on which was to be inscribed the following motto: "Liberty—Equality—Constitution of 1793—General Happiness." Whoever should resist the sovereign people was doomed to death. The bakers and wine-dealers were to furnish bread and liquids to the people, receiving an indemnity from the republic, under pain of being hanged at the lantern in case of refusal.

The true democratic republic which was to be thus ushered in by robbery and blood was to be one in which there should be neither rich nor poor, neither high nor low, but all should be equal. This, he maintained, could not be accomplished until all property came into the hands of the government, and was by it statedly divided amongst the citizens, giving to each one exactly the same proportion of the whole : practically working out a sum in long division, the divisor being the number of citizens. He desired a community of goods, and this was to be made enduring by the abolition of private property. The State, as sole proprietor, was to give to each his work according to his skill, and his subsistence according to his need. Any one who got more than he needed was guilty of theft. He advocated the removal of the surplus population, and, anticipating modern history, would remove the landlords first. Then the remainder might live in ease. He spoke of the Terror as an excellent means of promoting the welfare of the whole. He was confronted with the argument that civilization, the arts, the sciences, and literature might be destroyed. He recked not. "All evils," he said, " are on their trial. Let them all be confounded. Let everything return to chaos, and from chaos let there rise a new and regenerated world."

Socialism being now launched upon society, has visited every land. Just as a particular species of plant or of animal will in one land develop differently from the same species in another, influenced by the soil and climate, by the quantities of sunshine and of rain, so that in course of time differences will be so marked that really new species will have come into existence, yet retaining fundamental similarities; so has it been with Socialism. Socialism coming in contact with different national characteristics, differences of temperament and of disposition, with different social and economic conditions, and with different systems of religion and of government, has become sometimes comparatively mild and harmless, sometimes fiercely revolutionary and

destructive ; sometimes it has been thoughtful and scientific
sometimes ignorant, rash, and reckless ; sometimes it has
been imbued with a spirit that might almost be called
religious, and sometimes it has been animated by a spirit
rampantly and blasphemously atheistic.

Its fortunes have been various.   Sometimes it has been
welcomed, sometimes shunned, and sometimes persecuted.
In some places it has made progress at first, and then
seems to have languished ; in others it was at first coldly
received, and after some time gained many adherents ; and
again in other places making converts early, it continues
to advance.   The distribution of wealth, the pressure of
poverty, the prospects of material improvement, the attitude
of the government and of public opinion, the traditions
and spirit of the people, have generally determined its
success or failure.

In *Germany* Socialism made rapid progress, and is still
a great power ; the conditions were favourable to its growth.
"Dr. Engel, head of the Statistical Bureau of Prussia,
states that in 1875 six million persons, representing, with
their families, more than half the population of that State,
had an income less than twenty-one pounds a year each ;
and only one hundred and forty thousand persons had incomes above one hundred and fifty pounds.   The number of
landed proprietors is indeed comparatively large.   In 1861
there were more than two millions of them out of a population of twenty-three millions ; and in a country where
half the people are engaged in agriculture, this would, at
first sight, seem to offer some assurance of general comfort.
But then the estates of most of them are much too small to
keep them in regular employment, or to furnish them with

adequate maintenance. More than a million hold estates of less than three acres each, and averaging little over an acre, and the soil is poor. The consequence is that the small proprietor is almost always over head and ears in debt. His property can hardly be called his own, and he pays to the usurer a much larger sum annually as interest than he could rent the same land for in the open market."

Prince Bismarck, speaking of the spread of Socialism in a purely agricultural district like Lauenburg, which had excited surprise, said that this would not seem remarkable to any one who reflected that, from the land legislation in that part of the country, the labourers could never hope to acquire the smallest spot of ground as their own possession, and were kept in a state of dependence on the gentry and the peasant proprietors.

It is said that German workmen are discontented and improvident. They are also heavily taxed, and very seriously suffer from enforced military service. Often the ablest member of the family to earn wages, wages sorely needed, is taken away by conscription to serve in the army. Hence it is no matter of wonder that Socialism found in Germany congenial soil.

In tracing the historical development of a movement, we must not only consider its environment, but we must also consider the leading men who originated or formulated or taught it. In every movement of importance, we find particular men who impress their personality upon it, who voice the opinions and sentiments that are in a vague and semi-conscious state in the minds and hearts of thousands. They systematise ideas that have not been co-ordinated. They give expression to ideals that have

loomed as in a mist before the miud's eye. They modify
extravagant desires. They intensify languid feelings. They
give definiteness of aim. They provide " a local habitation
and a name " for the spirit or genius of the movement.
They become identified, almost incorporated with it. We
cannot think of the Reformation without thinking of
Martin Luther ; we cannot think of the Society of Jesus
without thinking of Ignatius Loyola ; we cannot think of
Methodism without thinking of John Wesley ; nor can we
think of Socialism without thinking of Ferdinand Lassalle
and Karl Marx.

CHAPTER II.

FERDINAND LASSALLE was born of Jewish parents in
comfortable circumstances at Breslau in the year 1825,
and was educated at the universities of Breslau and Berlin.
He became an enthusiastic Hegelian. He wrote articles
on it in magazines, had it " on the brain," and preached it
" in season and out of season." It is very important for
us to notice how men of thought influence men of action.
Those who are called practical men often overlook this, and
speak as if abstract thinkers exercised no real power over
human events. No greater mistake could be made. It is
likely that no one of the men whom we shall find to have
been powers in the socialistic movement exerted on that
movement more vital influence than the German philosopher, who never sat in a legislative chamber, and never
addressed a public meeting in his life. We shall find that
not only Lassalle, the originator of social democracy in
Germany, but Karl Marx, the founder of scientific Socialism,
and Bakunin, the apostle of Russian anarchism, drank in
eagerly the Hegelian philosophy.

George William Frederick Hegel was born at Stuttgart in
1770, and died of cholera in Berlin in his sixty-first year,

when Lassalle was six years old. He received a good
classical education in Würtemberg, and went to Tübingen
to study theology. His sermons were failures; however,
he got a theological certificate, which declared that he
was of "good abilities, middling industry, and especially
deficient in philosophy." Whilst he had not a brilliant
university career, he gathered immense stores of mis-
cellaneous knowledge, and made himself at home in the
Greek and Roman world.

Hunger impelled him to become a private tutor; but
on the death of his father in 1801, he got a small property
that enabled him to relinquish his tutorship, when he
removed to Jena. There he published his dissertation *De
Orbitis Planetarum*. In it Newton was treated with scorn
as an empiric. He ridicules Newton's device, "Physics
beware of metaphysics," by saying it might be translated
"Science beware of thought," and remarks that this precept
the followers of Newton have faithfully followed.

Hegel always treated with contempt those who trust to
facts, rather than to ideas evolved from their own consciousness. It is interesting to note that, whilst in this
dissertation he satisfactorily proves that there cannot be
a planet between Mars and Jupiter, before the ink was
dry Professor Piazzi had discovered the first of the asteroids,
thus showing how specious and how false an argument
may be when not based on discovered fact, how much
safer it is to trust ourselves to inductive rather than to
deductive logic.

He became *privat-docent* at the University of Jena.
Here his work was brought to an abrupt conclusion by the
battle of Jena. Like Archimedes at the siege of Syracuse,

he was so engrossed in his work that he continued writing his *Phänomenologie des Geistes,* undisturbed by the thunder of the artillery. Next morning French soldiers made him understand that he would have to give up writing books for a time—at least at Jena. How he viewed the public movements then in progress may be gathered from the close of his lectures on the phenomenology of the mind.

" This, gentlemen, is speculative philosophy as far as I have worked it out. We stand in a momentous time—a seething mass, in which the mind has made a sudden bound, left its old shape behind and is gaining a new. The whole bulk of our old ideas, the very bands of the world, are rent asunder, and collapse like a dream. Mind is preparing a new start. Philosophy, above all things, has to own and welcome such a start. While some in powerless resistance cling to the past, and the majority help, but unconsciously, to swell the numbers of its *cortége,* philosophy, recognising it as the eternal, has to show it due honour."

After various fortunes, teaching school, editing a newspaper, and getting happily married, he was called to a professor's chair in Heidelberg, and in two years after to one in Berlin, where he lectured for thirteen years, formed a school, produced his best works, and made many friends.

This professor, with his old-fashioned face without life or lustre, with a marvellous appetite for snuff, and so bad a delivery that every sentence, and almost every word, seemed to come out with a struggle, influenced in no ordinary degree the men who made Socialism.

We may very well ask, What was his philosophy? It

is not easy to give a summary of the teaching of eighteen large volumes in a paragraph or two. Especially is this the case with Hegel, for perhaps there is no great writer whose works are more difficult to understand. Scarcely two commentators are agreed as to what he meant to teach. To add to the difficulty of understanding an obscure style, he uses words in different senses.

Every one knows the legend which represents him as saying, " Only one of my pupils understood me," and then adding with a sigh, " and even he misunderstood me." But amongst all that is uncertain or ambiguous in his teaching, it is at any rate certain that he taught the doctrine of evolution. " That the absolute contains within itself, by the very necessity of its nature, a principle of evolution from difference to difference, which differences are its moments." " In the development of humanity we are told by Hegel that the races are moments. The negro race is the natural mind in itself; the Mongolian shows the mind conscious of its opposition to this natural form, and tending to rise above it; the Caucasian is the free mind—mind returned to the absolute unity in itself."

He shows in various ways the value of organization. He teaches distinctly the supremacy of philosophy over revelation. This has led one section of his followers to rank, materialistic atheism. Mr. Lewes in his valuable *History of Philosophy* says: " Remark also that this absolute idealism is Hume's scepticism in dogmatical form. Hume denied the existence of mind and matter, and said there was nothing but ideas. Hegel in effect denies the existence of both object and subject, since the only reality of either depends on its relation to the other."

He also taught the reality of necessary thoughts, a doctrine embodied in his well-known saying: " Whatever is rational is real, whatever is real is rational." Much of his teaching is expressed in the formula: " Thesis, antithesis, synthesis."

After this brief reference to the great teacher of absolute idealism, we return to Lassalle, his ardent disciple. After the dissolution of the first Prussian National Assembly in 1848, a constitution by royal decree was given to that country. This increased the discontent, and added to it the bitterness of disappointment, because the constitution was so much less liberal than had been hoped for by the people. A widespread agitation resulted, and a combination was formed to refuse to pay taxes until popular measures were conceded. At Düsseldorf, Lassalle planned an armed insurrection. The government immediately put the town under a state of siege, and imprisoned Lassalle.

At his trial he claimed the right of active resistance to the decrees of the State when they were not in accordance with the popular will, and condemned the policy of passive resistance.

" Passive resistance," he said, " is a contradiction in itself. It is like Lichtenberg's knife, with blade and without handle, or like the fleece which one must wash without wetting. It is mere inward ill-will without the outward deed. The Crown confiscates the people's freedom, and the Prussian National Assembly, for the people's protection, declares ill-will; it would be unintelligible how the commonest logic should have allowed a legislative assembly to cover itself with such incomparable ridicule, if it were not too intelligible."

He declared himself a "socialist Democrat," and asserted that he was revolutionary on principle. "Revolution," he says, "means merely transformation, and is accomplished when an entirely new principle is— either with force or without it—put in the place of an existing state of things. Reform, on the other hand, is when the principle of the existing state of things is continued, and only developed to more logical or just consequences. The means do not signify. A reform may be carried out by bloodshed, and a revolution in the profoundest tranquillity. The Peasants' War was an attempt to introduce reform by arms, the invention of the spinning-jenny wrought a peaceful revolution."

He had intended to qualify himself as a *privat-docent* at the University of Berlin; but instead of doing so, he devoted himself romantically, and with untiring energy, to the task of redressing the wrongs of the Countess Hatzfeldt. This lady was early married to an unsympathetic husband, a cruel and licentious man, who first neglected and then persecuted her.

Lassalle brought her case before thirty-six different courts, and succeeded in getting a divorce for her, after eight years of toil, in 1851, and then a large fortune in 1854, out of which she settled a considerable sum upon him, that produced an annual income of four thousand thalers, equal to about six hundred pounds. Till Lassalle's death she continued his warmest friend, and after his death was his most sincere mourner.

In showing how he was led to champion her cause, he says: "Her family were silent, but it is said when men keep silent the stones will speak. When every human right is

violated, when even the voice of blood is mute, and help-
less man is forsaken by his born protectors, there then
rises with right man's first and last relation—man. You
have all read with emotion the monstrous history of the
unhappy Duchess of Praslin. Who is there among you
that would not have gone to the death to defend her?
Well, gentlemen, I said to myself, here is Praslin ten
times over. What is the sharp death-agony of an hour
compared with the pangs of death protracted over twenty
years? What are the wounds a knife inflicts compared
with the slow murder dispensed with refined cruelty
throughout a being's whole existence? What are they
compared with the immense woe of this woman, every
right of whose life has been trampled under foot, day
after day, for twenty years, and whom they have first tried
to cover with contempt, that they might then the more
securely overwhelm her with punishment? The difficulties, the sacrifices, the dangers did not deter me. I
determined to meet false appearances with the truth, to
meet rank with right, to meet the power of money with
the power of mind. But if I had known what infamous
calumnies I should have to encounter, how people turned
the purest motives into their contraries, and what ready
credence they gave to the most wretched lies—well, I
hope my purpose would not have been changed, but it
would have cost me a severe and bitter struggle."

These trials brought Lassalle into public notice, and
his boldness, eloquence, and ability, as well as his popular
sympathies, soon made him a powerful influence in the
formation of public opinion.

He was, however, forbidden to enter Berlin. This he

felt as a great privation, as he believed that he could there best serve the cause he had at heart. Accordingly, one day in 1859, he entered it disguised as a wagoner, and, through the mediation of Alexander von Humboldt with the king, was permitted to remain.

In 1862, which we may regard as the beginning of the period of his social activity, he delivered a lecture to a working men's society in Berlin on "The Connexion between the present Epoch of History and the Idea of the Working Class." It was published in the following year. It states that there are three successive stages of evolution in modern history. First, the Feudal Period, when power was in the hands of the landowners, and was used for their benefit. Second, the Bourgeois Period, 1789–1848, when exclusive privileges were taken away from the nobles; power was held by landowners and the *bourgeois,* and was used by them to promote their own interests. Third, the Age of the Working Class; this period commenced in 1848, is not yet established, but is rapidly developing.

"What is the State?" asks Lassalle. "You are the State," he replies. "You are ninety-six per cent. of the population. All political power ought to be of you and through you and for you, and your good and amelioration ought to be the aim of the State. It ought to be so, because your good is not a class interest, but is the national interest."

He teaches that every man has a right to an existence worthy of his moral destiny, and that it is the duty of the State to secure that existence for him; that as no man should be enslaved, as no man should be ignorant, so no

man should be without property, as without property he
cannot enjoy his freedom or his education.

In his *Herr Bastiat-Schulze* he says: "The world is
now face to face with a new social question, the question
whether, since there is no longer any property in the
immediate use of another man, there should still exist
property in his mediate exploitation: *i.e.* whether the free
realization and development of one's power and labour
should be the exclusive private property of the owner of
the instruments and advances necessary for labour—*i.e.* of
capital; and whether the employer as such, and apart from
the remuneration of his own intellectual labour of management, should be permitted to have property in the value
of other people's labour—*i.e.* whether he ought to receive
what is known as the premium or profit of capital, consisting of the difference between the selling price of the
product and the sum of the wages and salaries of all
kinds of labour, manual and mental, that have contributed
to its production."

He maintains that all instruments of production should
be taken out of private hands and held collectively, as
well as all its products; that the property of the future
made by the working classes should belong to the working
classes, and that industry should be conducted on the
mutual instead of the proprietary principle.

He unsparingly condemns the present system as being
unjust to the labourer, who can never make more than a
bare subsistence. "The back of the labourer," he says, "is
the green table on which undertakers and speculators play
the game of fortune which production has become. It is
the green table on which they receive the heaps of money

thrown to them by the lucky *coup* of the roulette, and which they smite as they console themselves for an unlucky throw with the hope of better chances soon. The labourer it is who pays, with diminished work, with hard-earned savings, with entire loss of employment, and thus of the means of subsistence, for the failures entailed in this gambling of employers and speculators, whose false speculations and reckonings he has not caused, of whose greed he is not guilty, and whose good fortune he does not share."

"How is it the workman is so badly off when there is abundance all around ? Because of the 'iron economic law of wages,' according to which the average wages of labour always remain reduced to the subsistence necessary, conformably with a nation's standard of life, to the prolongation of existence, and to the propagation of the species."

"What," asked Lassalle once of a meeting of working men,—" what is the result of this law, which is unanimously acknowledged by men of science ? Perhaps you believe that you are men ? But economically considered you are only commodities. You are increased by higher wages like stockings, when there is a lack ; and you are again got rid of, you are, by means of lower wages—by what Malthus, the English economist, calls preventive and destructive checks—decreased like vermin, against which society wages war."

Contrasting the seller of labour, the working man, with the seller of other commodities, he points out that while the merchant, if he cannot get a fair price for his goods, can reserve them, the workman must sell his labour or starve.

Lassalle asserts that the State should take the workman out of this wretched condition, and therefore advocates that capital, and land, and means of communication, and banks, should be in the hands of the State. Lassalle was a national and not an international socialist, and believed that each State should settle its own social question for itself. He was also willing to try the formation of "productive associations," which, aided by the State, should gradually exploit the undertaker and the capitalist. Socialists however, as a whole, have not followed him in these two last-mentioned views. They seek for an international, not a national Socialism, and they desire an immediate rather than a gradual change.

He devoted himself with indomitable energy to the diffusion of those opinions. Having an open rupture with the Progressists, who were, whilst professedly Liberals, not sufficiently democratic for Lassalle, he wrote his open letter, which has been called the charter of German Socialism, drew up a working man's programme, and wrote his *Herr Bastiat - Schulze*, his largest economic work. Schulze was a leading member of the Progressist party, and Bastiat was the populariser in France of the orthodox political economy. Lassalle accused Schulze of being merely the echo of Bastiat, and therefore calls him "Bastiat-Schulze." The work is full of gross personalities, but presents some of Lassalle's views with much clearness and vigour. He spoke with great force, and often turned a hostile audience into a friendly and sympathetic one. The working men forsook Schulze and the Progressist party, and on May 23, 1863, Lassalle founded the "Universal German Working Men's Association" at Leipsic. He was elected president for five years, and in July, 1864, he had enrolled over four thousand members.

Lassalle, although the champion of the poor, and working with such energy, was of fashionable and luxurious habits. He was a connoisseur of wines. His suppers were exquisite entertainments. He liked to surround himself with what was rare in art and gay in society. His friend Heine, recognising his acuteness and power of expression and practical ability, at the same time says, " He is a genuine son of the new era, without even the pretence of modesty or self-denial, who will assert and enjoy himself in the world of realities." In some fashionable circle he met a young lady, Helena von Dönnigsen, accomplished and clever, but somewhat eccentric, and, like Lassalle himself, not at all disposed to be fettered by the conventionalities of society. After his severe labours, Lassalle went to Switzerland for much-needed rest, and again he met this young lady. He was most anxious to marry her; she was even more than willing. But her father, a German diplomatist, was decidedly opposed to it; so were all her friends, whose sympathies and interests were-bound up with the court party. At last, yielding to their persuasions, she gave up Lassalle and consented to marry Herr von Racowitza.

Lassalle sent a challenge to both father and bridegroom. The latter accepted it, and in the duel Lassalle was fatally wounded. A little less passion and vanity, and a little more saving common-sense and self-control, and he might have lived for many years. He died August 31, 1864, at the age of thirty-nine.

Many demonstrations were made as the body was taken

to Germany. His death caused much lamentation and woe. The mourners went about the streets. He was gathered to his fathers, and his remains repose in the Jewish burying-ground of his native place. Over his grave is the inscription : " Lassalle—Thinker and Fighter."

What, we may ask, was Lassalle's contribution to Socialism ? It is quite true that his plan of productive association with State credit has not been a practical success, whilst the co-operative societies founded by his great antagonist Schulze have proved to be an admirable means of improving the condition, and of giving valuable training to the working man. They have been contrasted as Self - help *versus* State - help. Yet Lassalle first led the Socialists to organize themselves as a distinct party, and made clear the fundamental difference between them and the Progressists in their idea of the functions of the State. According to the Progressists, the State was to be a "night watchman to prevent robbery and burglary." According to Lassalle, the State is to help in every way in procuring the development, culture, and happiness of the individual. Lassalle's statement of the "iron law of wages," by which far too small a portion of the produce of labour goes to the labourer, was his chief and special point in the economics of Socialism. This he endeavoured, with much force of reasoning and variety of illustration, to impress on his followers, and succeeded in convincing them that nothing less than an entire revolution in the existing industrial arrangements would give the worker that share of the means of enjoyment to which he is equitably entitled. This matter we shall consider further in another part of this lecture.

CHAPTER III.

WE have now to consider another and in many respects
a greater name. The man who has done more to make
Socialism what it is to-day than Lassalle, or any one else,
is Karl Marx. If Lassalle was the orator of Socialism,
Marx was its philosopher. Karl Marx is called the " Father
of scientific Socialism," and his great work on *Capital* is
called the " Socialists' Bible." As a student and thinker,
as an organizer and " man of affairs," he must be placed in
a high rank amongst the men who have made history in
the nineteenth century. Like Lassalle and many men of
mark, he was of Jewish blood, both his parents being of
that race.

He was born at Trèves,—famous for its holy coat,—in
the Rhine Provinces, on May 5, 1818. Originally the
name of the family was Mordecai—a name that suggests to
us unwavering devotion to the Hebrew God, the luxurious
Persian court, and the haughty Haman, who digged a pit
for another and fell into it himself. Karl's grandfather
changed the name to Marx.

When Trèves fell into the hands of Prussia, it is said
that the father of Karl Marx was offered the choice of

either renouncing his religion, or of giving up his profession as an advocate. He renounced Judaism, gained the favour of the Prussians, and obtained a good appointment under the government. It is possible that this incident may account for the bitterness with which Marx attacks Christianity, for it is certain that a religion thus forced by unworthy motives would raise a prejudice against itself on the part of every fair and candid mind.

Marx studied at Bonn, and Jena, and at Berlin; philosophy, political economy, and particularly history, attracted his attention. At the university he became, like Lassalle, an ardent Hegelian ; and this system of philosophy affected his mode of thought and of expression throughout his entire after life.

He was urged by his friends to adopt an academic career, and his marriage with the sister of Von Westfalen, a Prussian minister of state, would have helped in that sphere ; but just as he had finished his college course Friedrich Wilhelm IV. (1840) began to reign.

The Liberals of Germany thought that a new era would commence with the new king, that the day of liberty had dawned at last. In order to take an active part in promoting the reforms that were supposed to be at hand, Marx turned his attention to journalism, and joined the staff of the *Rhenish Gazette*, the organ of the " Young Hegelian " or " Philosophical Radical Party." The ability he displayed soon caused him to be appointed editor. His attacks on the government were so vigorous and telling, that a special censor was sent from Berlin to Cologne, and ultimately the journal was suppressed by the Prussian government in 1843. He then went to Paris, continued

The State must be humanized.   The sovereign people must
be both king and god.

"The princes are gods," says Feuerbach, "and they must
share the same fate.   The dissolution of theology into
anthropology in the field of thought is the dissolution of
monarchy into republic in the field of politics.   Dualism,
separation is the essence of theology ; dualism, separation is
the essence of monarchy.   There we have the antithesis of
God and world ; here we have the antithesis of State and
people."

Feuerbach's peculiar ethical principle has been called
" tuism " to distinguish it from " egoism."   " The nature of
man," he says, " is contained only in the community, in the
union of man with man.   Isolation is finitude and limitation, community is freedom and infinity.   Man by himself
is but man ; man with man, the unity of I and Thou, is
god."   The humanists, thus regarding the social man as the
true unit, were opponents of the individualistic basis of
society, and friends of its socialistic reconstruction.   Thus
through humanism Hegelians became Socialists.

There were, however, in many points considerable
divergences of opinion.   When they endeavoured to forecast the future social State, they differed.   They could agree
to pull down the present social system, but they could not
agree as to what they would build up in its place.   Therefore they gave themselves up to the work that divided
them least.

Marr, a humanist, says in his book on *Secret Societies in
Switzerland :* " The masses can only be gathered under the
flag of negation.   When you present detailed plans, you
excite controversies and sow divisions ; you repeat the

mistake of the French Socialists, who have scattered their redoubtable forces, because they tried to carry formulated systems. We are content to lay down the foundation of the revolution. We shall have deserved well of it, if we stir hatred and contempt against all existing institutions. We make war against all prevailing ideas of religion, of the State, of country, of patriotism. The idea of God is the keystone of a perverted civilization. It must be destroyed. The true root of liberty, of equality, of culture, is atheism. Nothing must restrain the spontaneity of the human mind."

Marx advanced with Feuerbach and became a humanist. He regarded humanism as the ferment that would leaven the social State of the future. " The new revolution," he says, " will be introduced by philosophy. The revolutionary tradition of Germany is theological. The Reformation was the work of a monk ; the revolution will be the work of a philosopher."

In the view of Marx it was the highest duty to destroy everything in the present order of things that makes man a degraded, insulted, forsaken, and despised being. In order to carry this out, the proletariat must unite and act. They have been oppressed and trampled upon. They are without property. They have been defrauded. In order that they may enjoy life and possess power, they must possess property. Private property must therefore cease.

"The only practical emancipation for Germany is an emancipation proceeding from the standpoint of the theory which explains man to be the highest being for man. In Germany the emancipation from the Middle Ages is only possible, as at the same time an emancipation from the partial conquests of the Middle Ages. In Germany one

kind of bond cannot be broken without all other bonds
being broken too.   Germany is by nature too thorough
to be able to revolutionise without revolutionising from a
fundamental principle, and following that principle to its
utmost limits; and therefore the emancipation of Germany
will be the emancipation of man.   The head of this
emancipation is philosophy, its heart is the proletariat."

In Paris, Marx also met *Friedrich Engels*, the most
intimate and trusted of all his companions, his "lifelong
and loyal friend and companion in arms."   Whilst Marx
was often engaged in conflicts with those of his own party,
or those who were nearly allied to his own party,—for in
Socialism, as in other systems, we see that "it is not the
colours that hate each other, but the shades," and in
Socialism there are many shades,—there was never any
difference or coolness between Marx and Engels.   They
were faithful to each other through good and bad report,
through good and evil fortune.   Amongst men prone to
suspicion and afflicted with that rottenness of the bones,
envy,—according to John Stuart Mill, the most anti-social
of all the vices,—neither envy nor suspicion ever marred
their friendship.   Marx, the philosophical journalist, and
Engels, the veteran Communist, worked together as if they
had entered into a solemn league and covenant.

On account of Marx's continued attacks in the press on
the Prussian government, he was expelled from Paris in
1845, and settled at Brussels.   There he wrote the *Misery
of Philosophy*, as an answer to Proudhon's *Philosophy of
Misery*, a proceeding which caused a final breach between
the two authors.   He also published a merciless criticism
on the medley of French-English Socialism and Com-

munism and German philosophy which then constituted
the secret doctrine of the Communist League, and insisted
that their work could have no tenable theoretical basis,
except that of a scientific insight into the economic structure of society, and that this ought to be put in a popular
form, not with the view of carrying out every utopian
system, but of promoting among the working and other
classes a self-conscious participation in the process of the
historical transformation of society that was taking place
under their eyes.

In order to carry this out, there ought to be a public
and vigorous propaganda of socialist principles, and a
wisely directed effort to educate public opinion in their
views.   The strictures of Marx were well taken.   A
congress was held in London, where a society of Socialists,
chiefly composed of German immigrants, had been established.   Marx and Engels were invited to be present,
and to draw up a "Manifesto of the Communist Party."
This was done in 1848.   It became the creed of the
International Socialists, and greatly enhanced the reputation of the two friends.   Instead of the old watchword,
" All men are brothers," it adopts a new one, " Proletarians
of all countries, unite ! "

The changes occurring in society are set forth in it;
the decay of feudalism, the supremacy of the *bourgeoisie*,
the condition of the proletariat, by far the largest section
of society, kept in poverty, without property or power or
anything worth calling a home.   It demands a republic,
the payment of members of Parliament, the conversion of
large estates, mines, etc., into State property, the appropriation by the State of all means of transport, such as

railways, canals, steamships, roads, and ports, the restriction of the law of succession, the introduction of a heavily graded income tax, the abolition of indirect taxation by abolishing excise duties, the establishment of national workshops, State guarantee to all work-people of an existence, and a provision for the incapable, universal and free education. As to the means of bringing all these changes about, the proletariat must gain political power, and possession of all property must be in the hands of the State.

The manifesto may be summed up as demanding—

(1) Expropriation of landed property, and application of rent to State expenditure; (2) Abolition of inheritance; (3) Confiscation of the property of all emigrants and rebels; (4) Centralization of credit in the hands of the State by means of a national bank, with State capital and exclusive monopoly; (5) Centralization of all means of transport in hands of State; (6) Institution of national factories, and improvement of lands on a common plan; (7) Compulsory obligation of labour upon all equally, and establishment of industrial armies, especially for agriculture; (8) Joint prosecution of agriculture and mechanical arts, and gradual abolition of the distinction of town and country; (9) Public and gratuitous education for all children, abolition of children's labour in factories, etc. The manifesto ends by saying: "The Communists do not seek to conceal their views and aims. They declare openly that their purpose can only be obtained by a violent overthrow of all existing arrangements of society. Let the ruling classes tremble at a communistic revolution. The proletariat have nothing to lose in it but their

chains ; they have a world to win. Proletarians of all
countries, unite ! "

During the revolution of 1848, Marx was expelled
from Brussels, and went by invitation of the provisional
government to Paris. After a few weeks, when the
German revolution broke out, he went to Cologne, and
there, with Engels and others, started the *New Rhenish
Gazette.* This journal urged the people to stop paying
taxes till the desired reforms were effected. It was
suppressed by the government after the Dresden insurrection was quelled. Its last number appeared in red type
in June, 1849, and contained Freilegrath's *Farewell of the
" New Rhenish Gazette "* :

> Farewell, but not for ever farewell !
> They cannot kill the spirit, my brother ;
> In thunder I'll rise on the field where I fell,
> More boldly to fight out another.
> When the last of crowns, like glass, shall break
> On the scene our sorrows have haunted,
> And the people its last dread " Guilty " shall speak, .
> By your side you shall find me undaunted.
> On Rhine or on Danube, in war and deed,
> You shall witness, true to his vow,
> On the wrecks of thrones, in the midst of the field,
> The rebel who greets you now.

After this Marx went to London, and devoted himself
to the study of economic questions, matured his views on
capital, was a constant reader in the British Museum
library, was correspondent for the *New York Tribune,* and
produced several pamphlets, one against Louis Napoleon,
another against Lord Palmerston, and another against a
fellow Socialist, Karl Vogt.

In 1864, Marx returned from his comparative retire-

ment, and once more took an active and conspicuous part
in public affairs.   Two years before, there had been the
International Exhibition of London, to which a deputation
of working-men came from France.   They were entertained
by some English working-men at the Freemasons' Tavern.
Their ideas regarding the identity of the interests of
labour, and the importance of united action for promoting
them, were interchanged.   In the following year another
deputation arrived, and the same subjects were discussed;
and then, in 1864, a public meeting of working-men of
different nationalities was held in St. Martin's Hall,
London.   A committee of fifty was appointed, about one-
half of them English, and commissioned to draw up a
constitution of the new association; and thus was founded
the most important, influential, and at one time most
dreaded of all socialistic associations, "The International
Working-men's Association."

Mazzini was connected with it at first.   He, however,
was too moderate; and as there was not much cordiality
between him and Marx, he soon retired from it, and ever
after used his influence against it.

Again Marx, who was the dominant influence and
practical founder of the association, urged as the watch-
word, "Proletarians of all countries, unite!"   It was declared
that the economic subjection of the labourer to the possessor of the means of labour, *i.e.* of the sources of life,
is the first cause of his political, moral, and material servitude, and that the economic emancipation of labour is
consequently the great aim to which every political
movement ought to be subordinated.

The International continued to be a revolutionary force,

and a name of dread, until the establishment of the Paris Commune, after the outbreak of the Franco-German war. If the leaders of the International did not actively promote the Commune, it is certain that they heartily approved of and deeply sympathised with it. Marx made no secret of his views on the subject. But its excesses led the English members to forsake the International, and at the congress at the Hague in 1872 it was divided into two strongly antagonistic parties.

One party was the Centralist Democratic Socialists, under the leadership of Marx ; and the other was the Anarchist Socialists, under the leadership of Michael Bakunin. The difference between these parties was of an exceedingly serious character.

The Centralist Democratic Socialists maintained that, under the scheme of collective property, co-operative production would only be possible under one great central authority, armed with sufficient power to enforce its decisions.

The Anarchist Socialists adopted the principle of Proudhon,—as we have seen, an old opponent of Marx, —that the true form of the State is anarchy : meaning by that, not disorder, but the absence of any supreme authority, either king, parliament, or convention, the absence of all control, and the management of property and all industrial enterprises by groups of working-men voluntarily associating themselves together.

After the fall of the International, Marx ceased to take an active part in public affairs, but devoted himself to the completion of his great work, *Das Kapital*, till his death, in Paris, in the spring of 1883.

His work on *Capital* consists of two large volumes. The first volume, published in 1867, treats of the "Production of Capital"; and the second, published in 1885, treats of its circulation. This work shows immense research, no fewer than three hundred and fifty English authors being quoted in it. It is characterized by keen analysis, and by a patient and profound investigation of the subject. It is spoken of by Socialists in terms of rapturous approval.

Dr. Aveling says of it: "That which Darwin did for biology, Marx has done for economics. Each of them by long and patient observation, experiment, recordal, reflection, arrived at an immense generalization,—a generalization the like of which their particular branch of science had never seen ; a generalization that not only revolutionised that branch, but is actually revolutionising the whole of human thought, the whole of human life. And that the generalization of Darwin is at present much more universally accepted than that of Marx, is probably due to the fact that the former affects our intellectual rather than our economic life—can, in a word, be accepted in a measure alike by the believers in the capitalistic system and by its opponents. There can be little doubt that the two names by which the nineteenth century will be known, as far as its thinking is concerned, will be those of Charles Darwin and Karl Marx."

Marx distinguishes between *utility* value and *exchange* value. Thus atmospheric air has great utility value, but no exchange value. On the other hand, a diamond has little utility value, but great exchange value. The difference is caused by labour: nothing in which labour is not solidified has exchange value. If there was no labour in getting diamonds, they would have no exchange value. The value is the labour materialised in any article.

He says: " As values in exchange all commodities are only definite masses of congested labour time," and " that a day's labour of given length always turns out a product of the same value."

He endeavours to show that capital cannot be made by the exchange of commodities. " Considered abstractly, or independently of circumstances which do not proceed from the inherent laws of the simple circulation of commodities, the act of exchange is, apart from the substitution of one use-value by another, merely a metamorphosis, a change of form in the commodities. The same value—that is, the same quantity of incorporated social labour — remains in the hand of each owner of the commodity : first, in the form of his commodity ; then in the form of money which it has assumed ; and, finally, of the commodity to which the money is again changed. This change of form does not imply a change in the magnitude of the value. But the change which the value of the commodity itself undergoes in this process is confined to a change of its money-form. This form exists, first, as the price of the commodity offered for sale ; then as a sum of money,—expressed, however, in the price already ; and, finally, as the price of an equivalent commodity. This change of form *per se* as little implies a change in the magnitude of the value as does the exchange of a five-pound note for sovereigns, half-sovereigns, and shillings. Thus, so far as the circulation of the commodity only implies a change in the form of its value, it implies, when the phenomenon takes place in a pure form, the exchange of equivalents."

"The formation of surplus value, and therefore the conversion of money into capital, can thus be explained neither by the assumption that the sellers dispose of their commodities above their value, nor that the buyers purchase them below their value."

Capital thus not arising from any of the processes. of exchange, whence then does it arise? Marx shows, or at least aims at showing, that it results from the exploitation of the labourer by the capitalist.

Labour, like every other commodity, has a utility value and an exchange value. The labourer does not get his utility value for his work, but only its exchange value, which is by the iron and necessary law of wages what will suffice to keep him; and the race of labourers and the difference between this and his utility value is taken by the capitalist. The labourer cannot insist on getting his utility value, because he must sell his labour or starve.

Labour may be divided into *socially necessary* labour and *surplus* labour.

Socially necessary labour is that which is necessary to keep the labourer, according to the ideas of what is necessary in his age and place. Suppose a labourer by working four hours can make what is necessary to keep him, then, if he works ten hours, four hours are socially necessary labour, and six hours are surplus labour. Again, suppose that a man working ten hours at a piece of leather, worth eight shillings, can make it, as shoes, worth eighteen shillings, and that he gets for his labour four shillings : there is thus created for the capitalist six shillings, the value of the surplus labour of the labourer.

Capital is thus created entirely by the labourer working for a longer time than he need work, in order to keep himself and to keep up a supply of labourers. It is therefore the constant aim of the capitalist to keep wages low and the hours of labour long, so that his capital may grow with ever-increasing velocity. Consequently there can be no peace between labour and capital.

" There is now," says Marx, " to be expropriated, not the independently working labourer, but the capitalist exploiting many labourers. This expropriation is effected by the working of the immanent laws of this very capitalist production, by the centralization of capital. One capitalist ever kills many. Hand in hand with this centralization, or the expropriation of many capitalists by few, are developed the co-operative form of the labour process,— and that on a constantly increasing scale,—the intelligent application of science to technical purposes, the systematic exploitation of the soil, the transformation of the means of labour into means of labour only usable in common, the economising of all means of production by their use for production by combined social labour, the entwining of all nations in the net of the world-market, and thus the international character of the capitalist *régime.* With the steady decrease of the capital magnates, who usurp and monopolise all the advantages of this process of transformation, the mass of want, oppression, servitude, degradation, and spoliation grows ; but the revolt of the labouring class —swelling ever in numbers, and disciplined, united, and organized by the mechanism of the capitalist process of

production itself—spreads at the same time. The capitalist
monopoly becomes a fetter on the mode of production with
and under which it has originated. The centralization of
the means of production and the socialization of labour
reach a point at which they become no longer compatible
with their capitalist integument, and this is burst asunder.
The last hour of capitalist private property strikes. The
expropriators are expropriated."

This expropriation of the expropriators is to be accomplished by any means, at any cost. He further says :

" It cannot be said that the social movement excludes
the political. There is no political movement that is not
at the same time social. Only by so ordering things that
there shall be no classes and no class distinctions, will
social evolutions cease to be political revolutions. Until
then, on the eve of every general reorganization of society
the final word of social science will always run, ' Combat
or death, bloody war or nothing.' There is the question
inexorably put."

Marx contends that industrial improvements—the use of
machinery and of labour-saving apparatus—are all against
the labourer and in favour of the capitalist. Machinery
enables more work to be done with less expenditure of
human labour, and so enables one man to do the work of
ten, which is equivalent to making him work so much
longer, and consequently there is so much more surplus
labour for the capitalist.

Machinery involving largely the work of mere superintendence, as in weaving factories, enables the cheaper
work of women and children to be used, so that the
capitalist can get the labour of an entire family for what

ought to be the value of the labour of the head of the household.

Machinery can go on for ever ; and the tendency of using it will always be to make those who have spent capital in acquiring it take more and more out of the labourer in order to make him keep pace with the machinery.

The contribution of Marx to Socialism was very great. The chief part, not by any means the entire of it, was his exposition of capital. In this he gives a scientific justification of the discontent of the labourer and of the demands of the Socialist. He endeavoured to show, with greater wealth of learning and greater power of analysis than Rodbertus or any other writer, that all capital was made by labour, and should belong to the labourers. His teaching on this subject is the orthodox doctrine of Socialists to-day, and is indeed the only legitimate justification of their economic ideas. Those ideas are built on the doctrines of Marx. In another part of this lecture we hope to show the absolute falseness of his doctrines ; and when the foundations are destroyed the superstructure must perish.

In sketching the lives of Lassalle and Marx, the history of Socialism in Germany has been necessarily delineated. It is, however, necessary to notice a very important congress held at Gotha in 1875, at which a programme was adopted that has been substantially the programme of the Democratic Socialists ever since. It consists of two parts, a part for the present and for the future ; or, as it has been said, of three parts, the programme for to-day, the programme for to-morrow, and the programme for the day after to-morrow.

THE GOTHA PROGRAMME.

" I. Labour is the source of all wealth and civilization ; and since productive labour as a whole is made possible only in and through society, the entire produce of labour belongs to society : that is, it belongs by an equal right to all its members, each according to his reasonable needs, upon condition of a universal obligation to labour.

" In existing society the instruments of labour are the monopoly of the capitalist class; the dependence of the labouring class which results therefrom is the cause of misery and servitude in all forms.

" The emancipation of labour requires the conversion of the instruments of labour into the common property of society, and the management of labour by association, and the application of the product with a view to the general good, and an equitable distribution.

" The emancipation of labour must be the work of the labouring class, in relation to which all other classes are only a reactionary mass.

" II. Starting from these principles, the Socialistic Labour Party of Germany seeks by all lawful means to establish a free State and a socialistic society, to break asunder the iron law of wages by the abolition of the system of wage-labour, the suppression of every form of exploitation, and the correction of all political and social inequality.

" The Socialistic Labour Party of Germany, although at first working within national limits, is sensible of the international character of the labour movement, and is resolved to fulfil all the duties thereby laid on working men, in order to realize the brotherhood of all men.

" The Socialistic Labour Party of Germany demands, in order to pave the way for the solution of the social question, the establishment by State help of socialistic productive associations under the democratic control of the workpeople. Productive associations for industry and agriculture should be created to such an extent that the socialistic organization of all labour may arise out of them.

" The Socialistic Labour Party of Germany demands as the basis of the State : (1) Universal, equal, and direct suffrage, together with secret and obligatory voting, for all citizens over twenty years of age, in all elections in State and commune. The election day must be a Sunday or holiday. (2) Direct legislation by the people. Decision on peace or war by the people. (3) Universal liability to military service. Militia instead of standing army. (4) Abolition of all exceptional laws, especially laws interfering with liberty of the press, of association, and of meeting ; in general, all laws restricting free expression of opinion, free thought, and free enquiry. (5) Administration of justice by the people. Gratuitous justice. (6) Universal, compulsory, gratuitous, and equal education of the people by the State. Religion to be declared a private affair.

" The Socialistic Labour Party of Germany demands within the conditions of existing society : (1) The utmost possible extension of political rights and liberties in the sense of the above demands. (2) The replacement of all existing taxes, and especially of indirect taxes, which peculiarly burden the people, by a single progressive income tax for State and commune. (3) Unrestricted right of combination. (4) A normal working day corresponding to the needs of society. Prohibition of Sunday

4

labour. (5) Prohibition of the labour of children, and of all labour for women that is injurious to health and morality. (6) Laws for protection of the life and health of workmen. Sanitary control of workmen's dwellings. Inspection of mines, factories, workshops, and home industry by officers chosen by working-men. An effective Employers' Liability Act. (7) Regulation of prison labour. (8) Entire freedom of management for all funds for the assistance and support of working-men."

The phrase " by lawful means " was left out from the first paragraph of the second part of the Wyden Conference of 1880, in consequence of the anti-socialist laws that were passed because of the Socialist attempts on the life of the Emperor William in 1878, and was not reinserted at the Halle Conference of 1891.

Minor modifications were made, as, for example, asking for an eight hours' instead of a ten hours' day, thirty-six hours' continuous and uninterrupted rest, instead of the Sunday rest; but the changes were so slight that we may regard the Gotha programme as a full and accurate expression of the demands of Democratic Socialism.

The violent section in Germany is not sufficiently strong to form a separate party. Some of them were expelled in 1880 and others in 1891, when they urged an earnest crusade against the Church and religion. They were answered by Leibknecht.

" Instead," said he, " of squandering our strength in a struggle with the Church and sacerdotalism, let us go to the root of the matter. We desire to overthrow the State of the classes. When we have done that, the Church and sacerdotalism will fall with it; and in this respect we are much more radical and much more definite in purpose than our opponents, for we like neither the priests nor the anti-priests."

The Democratic Socialists are a powerful party in Germany; at the general election this year 1893 they returned forty-four members to the Reichstag, being an increase of eight over the number returned at the election of 1890. They polled four hundred thousand votes more than the Ultramontanes, who in 1890 ran them very close. They are thus the numerically strongest party in the empire, and during the last three years have increased about twenty-two per cent.

Besides the Democratic Socialists of Germany, there are three modifications of Socialism of sufficient importance to demand our attention.

CHAPTER IV.

CHRISTIAN SOCIALISM.—There are two developments of Christian Socialism that we must examine, one in Germany and another in England. We shall examine Christian Socialism in Germany now, and defer the examination of Christian Socialism in England, until we consider the development of Socialism in that country.

There was an element of Christian Socialism in the system of Saint-Simon. He was a French noble, and in his last work, *Nouveau Christianisme* (1825), he teaches that the principle of Christian fraternity should lead all classes above the lowest " to labour for the development, material, moral, and intellectual, of the class the most numerous and the poorest." In order that this might be accomplished, he argued that there must be a radical reform of the institution of property and inheritance.

Many connected with the Churches looked on Socialism as being one of those evil things which have in them a " soul of goodness," and believed that, if it could be purged of its atheism and antitheism, materialism and revolutionary elements, it might be made a valuable instrument for the elevation of humanity. They were disposed to accept the theory of value propounded by Marx, and to aid in securing a higher standard of living for the working-man.

Dr. Döllinger, a high authority in the Church of Rome before the dogma of the Papal infallibility had been pronounced, afterwards the head of the Old Catholic movement, recommended the Catholic clubs of Germany to discuss the question, so that a socialism under the guidance and benediction of the Church might prevail.

William Immanuel Baron von Ketteler, Bishop of Mayence, a man of high rank and immense energy, wrote a pamphlet, in which he declared: "It is no longer possible to doubt that the whole material existence of almost the entire labouring population,—*i.e.* of much the greatest part of men in modern States, and of their families,—that the daily question about the necessary bread for man, wife, and children, is exposed to all the fluctuations of the market and of the price of commodities. I know nothing more . deplorable than this fact. What sensations must it cause in those poor men who, with all they hold dear, are day after day at the mercy of the accidents of market price ? That is the slave market of our Liberal Europe, fashioned after the model of our humanist, rationalistic, antichristian Liberalism and freemasonry."

He also advocated that the Church should voluntarily raise a large sum of money to be used for starting productive associations, and that these associations should be both carried on and owned by working-men.

Moufang, another ecclesiastic, is more disposed to lean on the State to aid industrial undertakings than on voluntary contributions, and advocates that the State should protect the working-man against injurious surroundings—working too long and for too little remuneration ; also that it ought to reduce the taxes and military burdens of the working classes.

Many clubs, called Christian Social Associations, or from the name of their patron saint, himself a working-man, St. Joseph Associations, exist to carry out those views. By their means many hope to preserve the working-men in the Church of Rome, and to save them from the objectionable principles and practices of the Social Democrats.

More than ten years after the Roman Catholic Christian socialistic movement began, a similar one was instituted by Protestants. They thought that, whilst Democratic Socialists and Roman Catholic Socialists were manifesting such anxiety to improve the condition of the working-man, it was neither wise nor becoming for Protestants to appear indifferent to his interests. Many of them also seem to have been convinced of the truth of the economic theories of Marx and Lassalle.

Pastor Rudolph Todt, in his work on *Radical German Socialism and Christian Society*, maintains that the New Testament is an authoritative guide on economic questions. He condemns the present system of capitalistic production, and maintains that there is a close affinity between Christianity and Socialism, insomuch that "every merely nominal Christian is a spiritual Manchestrist worshipping *laisser faire* with his whole soul, and that a Manchestrist is never a true Christian."

His analysis of Democratic Socialism is that it consists of three elements : first, in economics, communism ; second, in politics, republicanism ; and third, in religion, atheism.

He accepts its first and second elements, communism and republicanism, but regards its third, atheism, as a mistake, and seems inclined to think that, if Socialists adopted Christianity instead of atheism, their triumph would be immediate and complete.

Amongst the Evangelicals who have joined the movement, a foremost place must be allotted to Dr. Stöcker, court preacher at Berlin. At an International Conference of the Evangelical Alliance, held in Florence in 1891, he said: " With the exception of a few narrow-minded believers, we all desire that that which is good in the aims of the social democracy should be accomplished; but no reasonable person approves of the evil objects among them, anarchy, unbelief, annihilation of personal liberty, and the destruction of family life.

"A change in men's thoughts has plainly come about. The Manchester School is no longer followed. The reign of Socialism has begun. Fundamentally it is a Christian law which is reorganized, the royal law of love, which for eighteen centuries all believers have obeyed in thought if not in practice. The Manchester School of political economy has done a good work in its time, especially in the direction of personal liberty and development of human energy and talent in connexion with natural forces, thus giving an immense impulse to economic life; but the principle of it was *individualism*. We see now the insufficiency of it, and all society is filled with the *social* spirit. The abstract humanity of Rousseau, with its idea of individual contract at the root of the State, is gone. The Church which Voltaire attacked with his sarcasm, and Lessing with his rationalism, is no longer a citadel of truth, but a ruin. Economical science in those days had for its motto, ' Laisser faire,' ' laisser aller.' The optimism which came from the school of Leibnitz, and believed that the best of all possible worlds would come out of forces left entirely to themselves, is passed away as a dream. The result of such a development of individual power has been seen to be egoism and mammonism—a materialism which, while it gathered the fruits of men's labour, neglected their personal and family life. Hence the terrible war of classes and interests which has ensued. In Germany, science has renounced the old theories, and the consequence is that they have been abandoned in practice. Economic individualism has proved itself an utter failure."

There are now various organizations under Protestant influences labouring for the elevation of the working classes. These associations differ more or less amongst themselves on the measure of aid to be received from the State, on the extent to which individuals should be permitted to hold private property, and to what extent the property of deceased persons should be taxed. On the whole, however, they accept the practical programme of the Democratic Socialists, divested of its atheistic and revolutionary elements.

These Christian Socialists have not been at all successful in gaining the confidence of the Democratic Socialists, whilst the bulk of the Reformed Churches regard and denounce them, as neither sound interpreters of Holy Scripture, nor loyal to their religious principles.

SOCIALISTS OF THE CHAIR.—The term *Katheder-Social-istens* was first used by Oppenheim in 1872, to designate and ridicule certain professors who to a large extent sympathised with the views and sentiments of Lassalle, yet were opposed to the German free trade or Manchester party, as well as to the Democratic Socialists.

These professors called together a congress at Eisenach in October, 1872, at which were prominent politicians, professors of economic science at the German universities, leaders of working-men, and large capitalists. A number of papers on factory legislation, trades unions, strikes, labourers' dwellings, and cognate subjects were read and amply discussed. At this congress, Professor Schmolle, for himself and his friends, like the disciples at Antioch, accepted the designation first given iu contempt, and by it they have since been specifically known.

These Socialists of the Chair belong to the historical school of political economists. This school studies what nations have thought, willed, and discovered in the economic field, what they have striven after, what they have attained to, and by what means and under what conditions they have attained it. They do not confine their attention to a number of contemporaneous facts, but view matters in their historical development. Hence they see how an economic system, at one time good and serviceable, may be unwise and inexpedient at a different stage of social culture. They are opposed to the theory of cosmopolitanism— that is, that there is an economic system equally adapted to every country; and to perpetualism—that is, that there is a system applicable to every social stage.

The Socialists of the Chair insist on the necessity of accentuating the moral element in economic study. They repudiate self-interest as the sole economic force, and point out that other forces—the sense of justice, the obligations of religion, individual and national idiosyn-

expresses a morbid, not a normal condition. The sound mind in a sound body desires to mingle with men and to act its part in the great drama of human life.

Society is not to be regarded as a mere accumulation of separate and distinct individuals coming into contact with each other, as grains of sand on the ocean shore, without having any vital bond of union between them. It is rather to be regarded as an organism, past, present, and future vitally connected together, all influencing each and each influencing all. As in the body, if one member suffers all the members suffer with it, if one member rejoices all rejoice with it, if one member—say the brain or the heart —does not fulfil its function, the whole body is injured; so in society, those who do wrong or who fail in doing their duty injure the whole, and those who do right, who faithfully perform their allotted task, benefit the whole. The welfare, or the reverse, of society is thus determined by the character and conduct of the individuals who compose it, as the condition of any aggregate will be determined by that of its component parts.

The condition of society will then just vary as the characters of the units that compose it varies. When men individually are selfish and licentious, false and full of greed, heedless of their duty to God and the rights of their fellows; when men are " like a vase of Egyptian asps, each one trying to get its head above the others " : then there will be oppression and discontent, unlawful gains and poverty, honest and dishonest, squalor in rags and luxury in purple, envy on the one hand and pride on the other, mutual distrust and mutual hatred. This condition may become so aggravated that a revolution is the inevitable result, or it may be so modified by the number of honest, unselfish, brotherly men—who are " the salt of the earth " —that society is preserved from dissolution, and normal development ensues.

At various periods in the history of the world, when the state of society has been well-nigh intolerable, men with a strong sense of justice, a hatred of oppression, deep sympathy with the suffering masses, or motives not so creditable, have stood forth as social reformers. Not always have social reformers been wise in their generation. It is true that often they have very clearly and indeed powerfully pointed out the existing evils; yet their proposals have been sometimes utopian and impracticable, and sometimes plausible but injurious, inasmuch as whilst removing some evils they would introduce other and worse ones. Then we have had social reformers who spoke the words of truth and soberness, and whose remedies were potent to purge the body politic of its malady and bring it to perfect soundness.

At the head of all social reformers we place Jesus of Nazareth. The period of His birth was one of exceptional darkness. " Darkness covered the earth, and gross darkness the peoples." Ever since the Dayspring from on high visited us has the day been growing brighter.

When Christ was born, in the Roman world it was an age of unbelief. Julius Cæsar, the chief pontiff of Rome, in his speech against Catiline, objected to his being put to death, on the ground that "death is a rest from troubles to those in grief and misery, not a punishment; it ends all the evils of life, for there is neither care nor joy beyond it." Here we have an official and deliberate denial of the immor-

tality of the soul. Men had ceased to have any real belief
in the gods. " To the multitude all religions were equally
true, to the magistrate all equally useful, and to the philosopher all equally false." Unbridled lust and cruelty prevailed. Prisoners were tortured Tens of thousands of
men were held in slavery ; and whilst the man who killed
a ploughing ox was punished, he who killed a slave of his
own was called to no account whatever. Beggars herded
together in crowds, and on their appeals for charity were
repelled with scorn. No one of all the rich men living in
luxurious Roman villas ever founded an asylum for the
poor or a hospital for the sick. Morals were so depraved,
that noble Roman matrons, in order to avoid the penalties
for adultery, enrolled themselves on the lists of public
prostitutes.

In Judæa, the Holy Land, relentless faction, gross licentiousness, unscrupulous avarice, heartless neglect and oppression of the poor, with the added evil of hypocrisy, marked
the degenerate sons of Abraham, who boasted of him as
their father, but whose sublime and simple faith they did
not inherit.

Into this world of unbelief and immorality, of cruelty
and wretchedness, Jesus came. He came as a great theological teacher, telling men of God, and of the eternal future,
and of duty. He came to give men an example of holy
living, to present His abstract doctrine of duty in concrete
form. He came, in order that by His sacrificial death He
might make " a full, perfect, and sufficient sacrifice, oblation,
and satisfaction for the sins of the whole world." But He
came in addition as a great social reformer.

The common people heard Him gladly. Why ? Not

altogether because they were attracted and impressed by His miracles, not altogether because His earnest and straightforward teaching appealed to their nature, less conventional than that of the ruling classes or the priestly caste, not altogether because they were dissatisfied with their condition and eager for novelty, but because they felt that He was their friend, that amidst neglect—as sheep without a shepherd—He was on their side and took their part.

And they were right. He was the friend of the poor, and the afflicted, and the downtrodden, and the outcast. He condemns the sins of those who had wealth and power. "Woe unto you, scribes and Pharisees, hypocrites! for ye devour widows' houses, and for a pretence make long prayers: therefore ye shall receive the greater damnation. . . . Woe unto you, scribes and Pharisees, hypocrites! for ye pay tithe of mint and anise and cummin, and have omitted the weightier matters of the law, judgment, mercy, and faith: these ought ye to have done, and not to leave the other undone. . . . Woe unto you, scribes and Pharisees, hypocrites! for ye make clean the outside of the cup and of the platter, but within they are full of extortion and excess. . . . Woe unto you, scribes and Pharisees, hypocrites! for ye are like unto whited sepulchres, which indeed appear beautiful outward, but are within full of dead men's bones, and of all uncleanness."

No wonder the common people heard gladly one who could thus speak, and with no " bated breath and whispering humbleness " could thus speak out against the evildoers and frauds and oppressors of His day. Jesus of Nazareth is the greatest of social reformers, and the system

He taught, if cast into the bitter well of our humanity, will make the waters sweet. Christianity—and by that word we understand the system of faith and morals taught by Jesus and His apostles, and contained in the New Testament—Christianity when regarded, not merely as a theory or a sentiment, as a something to discuss or to admire, but received by a living faith and made by that faith an operating power in the entire life, is capable of healing the deadly plague of society, and of enabling men to live a fully developed, well rounded, and joyous life, even in this world of sin and death.

Now there is another system which claims to have a deep sympathy with the poor and the suffering, and declares itself able to remove all social evils, and to solve all social problems, and to so reconstruct society that men shall lead lives free from the cares and troubles of the present, and with full satisfaction to themselves. This system is Socialism, and we are to consider it particularly in its relation to Christianity.

These two systems are gravely dissimilar in origin, in principles, in aims, in methods, and in motives.

It is true that there is some ground common to both. To a certain extent they overlap. That Socialist writers and leaders have consciously or unconsciously derived sentiments and ideas from Christianity is certain. Yet, because of this common ground, to represent the two systems as similar, or as allied, or as closely related to each other, is a mistake. We have been told that every Christian is a bit of a Socialist, and that every Socialist is a bit of a Christian. Now, would any one say that because there is some ground common to Christianity and to

Mohammedanism, therefore every Christian is a bit of a
Mohammedan, and every Mohammedan is a bit of a
Christian ?

Sometimes the difference between the two systems is
minified in order that Socialists may be gained to Christianity. To try to make a convert of a Socialist by
telling him that there is but little difference between
Socialism and Christianity, is not compatible with "simplicity and godly sincerity," and may only lead to disappointment and increased antagonism, when Christianity
is more fully known and the artifice discovered. No one
likes to be caught with guile. Here as elsewhere "honesty
is the best policy."

On the other hand, for a Christian who may be an
earnest philanthropist and impatient of surrounding evils,
who is not perhaps sufficiently considerate of the perplexity of life, who would like to see less inequality in the
distribution of wealth, hastily to call himself a Socialist,
may bring him into very strange company, and lead him to
feel, when he discovers the principles and practices of his
new associates, that he has made a mistake and must retrace
his steps, or become the subject of perpetual misunderstandings, or else—worst of all!—he may gradually lose his hold
of Christianity, and let the worse creed cast out the better.

Deep pity, earnest desire, and practical effort for the
amelioration of the hard lot of the poor man, with his
dependent family, out of employ, or of the poor man
struggling on under a heavy burden, and receiving what
are called, and sometimes rightly called, "starvation
wages," may be experienced by those who are not, as well
as by those who are, Socialists. The theories of Herbert

Spencer and of the Socialists are at opposite poles, yet he writes sympathetically and well :

" The fates of the great majority have ever been, and doubtless still are, so sad that it is painful to think of them. Unquestionably the existing type of social organization is one which none who cares for their kind can contemplate with satisfaction ; and unquestionably men's activities accompanying this type are far from being admirable. The strong divisions of rank and the immense inequalities of means are at variance with that ideal of human relations on which the sympathetic imagination likes to dwell ; and the average conduct under the pressure and excitement of social life, as at present carried on, is in sundry respects repulsive."

There are a large number of men who believe that many things under the present *régime* are unjust and ought to be changed, that laws should wisely promote the diffusion of wealth and not its extreme concentration, that the active business and not the idle interest should be favoured, that as in the family the weak one is taken special care of, so in the State those who are unable to take care of themselves ought to be efficiently protected. There are many who believe that labour ought to get its full reward, that men by associating themselves together should help one another and accomplish by co-operation what they could never accomplish without it, that the State may be rightly called upon to help society by doing whatever can be done better by State organization than by private enterprise. Yet these men are not Socialists, and distinctly repudiate the name as well as the principles and methods of Socialism. As the author of *Papacy, Democracy, and Socialism* says :

" It is right that words should preserve the sense which usage has given them, not only to enable us to understand one another when we speak, but also because it is not right that the defenders and the enemies of home and property should assume the same name, and should, even apparently, adopt the same colours, or march under the same flag. It is not possible to disarm revolutionary passions and refute submissive doctrines by borrowing their vocabulary ; on the contrary, if you take the name, you may often be compelled to submit to the thing."

We want then to answer, with as much accuracy as possible, the following questions : What is Socialism ? what are the principles that dominate it ? what are the objects at which it aims ? what are the methods that it is ready to use ? what are the motives by which it is inspired ?

Now, in order to do this, we must trace the historical development of Socialism, and in doing so we shall endeavour to let leading Socialists express their own opinions in their own language regarding this, as a much fairer method than that of paraphrasing their opinions ; for nothing is easier, even with every wish to be fair, than to misrepresent an opponent.

Socialists tells us that Socialism is the last word of the Revolution of 1789, and that the movement then begun must sooner or later end in a democratic communism. Before the French Revolution, oppression, which makes a wise man mad, had reached a point at which it was no longer endurable. Life was not worth living—so far as the masses were concerned. The few revelled in luxury, in licentiousness, in wanton cruelty and insolence. The many toiled hard, and had a meagre subsistence. Neither their humanity nor their citizenship was respected. Law permitted a seigneur, as he returned from hunting, to kill not more than two serfs, that he might refresh his feet in their warm blood. A keen sportsman amuses himself by shooting down plumbers and slaters, and sees them roll from their roofs with more gratification than if he had brought down an equal number of partridges or grouse.

Then these superiors, cruel, wanton, luxurious, were in general devoid of qualities calculated to gain the affection, the confidence, the admiration, or even the fear of the populace.

The masses, treated as beings who had duties but had no rights, who were the despised instruments of their superiors' greed, or ambition, or pleasure, conceived, as might be expected, a burning and bitter class hatred. They rose in rebellion, and, returning ferocity for ferocity and scorn for scorn, overturned the then existing social order. King and queen, nobles, clergy, and gentry, as well as many of the *bourgeoisie,* perished in the " Terror."

In what is probably his best work, Carlyle, speaking of the forces that caused this Revolution, says: " Powerfulest of all, least recognised of all, a Noblesse of Literature ; without steel on their thigh, without gold in their purse, but with the ' grand thaumaturgic faculty of Thought' in their head. French Philosophism has arisen ; in which little word how much do we include ! Here, indeed, lies properly the cardinal symptom of the whole widespread malady. Faith is gone out; Scepticism is come in."

Modern Socialism was generated out of the notions about property, and the State, and the origin and objects of civil

society maintained by these philosophers. They are proclaimed about the same period by many able writers: by
Brissot, by Malby, by Morelly, and above all by Rousseau.
Their leading thought was to restore what they called the
state of nature, when primitive equality still reigned, and
the earth belonged to none, but the fruits of it to all,
when there was common possession and common enjoyment. They taught that there was no foundation for property but need. He who needed a thing had a right to
it, and he who had more than he needed was a thief.
Rousseau said every man had naturally a right to whatever
he needed; and Brissot, anticipating the famous words of
Proudhon, declared that in a state of nature "exclusive
property was theft." It was so in a state of nature, but it
was so also in a state of society; for society was built on a
social contract, "the clauses of which reduce themselves to
one, *viz.* the total transfer of each associate, with all his
rights, to the community." This makes the individual
nothing, it makes the State everything. Property is only
so much of the national estate, conditionally conceded to the
individual. He has the right to use it because the State
permits him, while the State permits him, and how the
State permits him. So with every other right; he is to
think, speak, train his children as the State directs and
allows, in the interest of the common good. Thus objecting
to one slavery, they seek another and a worse one, and
entirely forget that the object of society ought to be to
protect natural rights, and not to *destroy* them.

These ideas remained as nebulous hypotheses till they
were systematised by Joseph Babœuf. He edited a journal
at Amiens, and ardently supported the Revolution, was

twice tried on account of the violence of his writing, but
was acquitted.   He joined a secret society, whose plans
were divulged by one of the members, and was condemned
for conspiracy to be guillotined.   On hearing the sentence
he stabbed himself, but was borne bleeding and dying to the
scaffold in May, 1797.   Such was the end of the man who
may most justly be called the father of modern Socialism.

Some four years before this tragedy, in 1793, Babœuf
discarded his Christian name of Joseph, because, as he said,
he did not desire the virtues of Joseph, took the name of
Caius Gracchus, and organized the conspiracy of the Egaux.
Then modern Socialism began.   He conducted an incendiary journal called *The Tribune of the People*, and in it
promulgated his views.   His desire was to form a true
democratic republic, which was to be brought about by the
diffusion of his views in his paper, and chiefly by the action
of his secret society.   At the appointed time the patriots
were to muster, with banners flying, on which was to be
inscribed the following motto: " Liberty—Equality—
Constitution of 1793—General Happiness."   Whoever
should resist the sovereign people was doomed to death.
The bakers and wine-dealers were to furnish bread and
liquids to the people, receiving an indemnity from the
republic, under pain of being hanged at the lantern in case
of refusal.

The true democratic republic which was to be thus
ushered in by robbery and blood was to be one in which
there should be neither rich nor poor, neither high nor
low, but all should be equal.   This, he maintained, could
not be accomplished until all property came into the
hands of the government, and was by it statedly divided

amongst the citizens, giving to each one exactly the same proportion of the whole : practically working out a sum in long division, the divisor being the number of citizens. He desired a community of goods, and this was to be made enduring by the abolition of private property. The State, as sole proprietor, was to give to each his work according to his skill, and his subsistence according to his need. Any one who got more than he needed was guilty of theft. He advocated the removal of the surplus population, and, anticipating modern history, would remove the landlords first. Then the remainder might live in ease. He spoke of the Terror as an excellent means of promoting the welfare of the whole. He was confronted with the argument that civilization, the arts, the sciences, and literature might be destroyed. He recked not. " All evils," he said, " are on their trial. Let them all be confounded. Let everything return to chaos, and from chaos let there rise a new and regenerated world."

Socialism being now launched upon society, has visited every land. Just as a particular species of plant or of animal will in one land develop differently from the same species in another, influenced by the soil and climate, by the quantities of sunshine and of rain, so that in course of time differences will be so marked that really new species will have come into existence, yet retaining fundamental similarities ; so has it been with Socialism. Socialism coming in contact with different national characteristics, differences of temperament and of disposition, with different social and economic conditions, and with different systems of religion and of government, has become sometimes comparatively mild and harmless, sometimes fiercely revolutionary and

destructive; sometimes it has been thoughtful and scientific
sometimes ignorant, rash, and reckless; sometimes it has
been imbued with a spirit that might almost be called
religious, and sometimes it has been animated by a spirit
rampantly and blasphemously atheistic.

Its fortunes have been various. Sometimes it has been
welcomed, sometimes shunned, and sometimes persecuted.
In some places it has made progress at first, and then
seems to have languished; in others it was at first coldly
received, and after some time gained many adherents; and
again in other places making converts early, it continues
to advance. The distribution of wealth, the pressure of
poverty, the prospects of material improvement, the attitude
of the government and of public opinion, the traditions
and spirit of the people, have generally determined its
success or failure.

In *Germany* Socialism made rapid progress, and is still
a great power; the conditions were favourable to its growth.
"Dr. Engel, head of the Statistical Bureau of Prussia,
states that in 1875 six million persons, representing, with
their families, more than half the population of that State,
had an income less than twenty-one pounds a year each;
and only one hundred and forty thousand persons had incomes above one hundred and fifty pounds. The number of
landed proprietors is indeed comparatively large. In 1861
there were more than two millions of them out of a population of twenty-three millions; and in a country where
half the people are engaged in agriculture, this would, at
first sight, seem to offer some assurance of general comfort.
But then the estates of most of them are much too small to
keep them in regular employment, or to furnish them with

adequate maintenance. More than a million hold estates of less than three acres each, and averaging little over an acre, and the soil is poor. The consequence is that the small proprietor is almost always over head and ears in debt. His property can hardly be called his own, and he pays to the usurer a much larger sum annually as interest than he could rent the same land for in the open market."

Prince Bismarck, speaking of the spread of Socialism in a purely agricultural district like Lauenburg, which had excited surprise, said that this would not seem remarkable to any one who reflected that, from the land legislation in that part of the country, the labourers could never hope to acquire the smallest spot of ground as their own possession, and were kept in a state of dependence on the gentry and the peasant proprietors.

It is said that German workmen are discontented and improvident. They are also heavily taxed, and very seriously suffer from enforced military service. Often the ablest member of the family to earn wages, wages sorely needed, is taken away by conscription to serve in the army. Hence it is no matter of wonder that Socialism found in Germany congenial soil.

In tracing the historical development of a movement, we must not only consider its environment, but we must also consider the leading men who originated or formulated or taught it. In every movement of importance, we find particular men who impress their personality upon it, who voice the opinions and sentiments that are in a vague and semi-conscious state in the minds and hearts of thousands. They systematise ideas that have not been co-ordinated. They give expression to ideals that have

loomed as in a mist before the mind's eye.   They modify
extravagant desires.   They intensify languid feelings.   They
give definiteness of aim.   They provide " a local habitation
and a name " for the spirit or genius of the movement.
They become identified, almost incorporated with it.   We
cannot think of the Reformation without thinking of
Martin Luther ; we cannot think of the Society of Jesus
without thinking of Ignatius Loyola ; we cannot think of
Methodism without thinking of John Wesley ; nor can we
think of Socialism without thinking of Ferdinand Lassalle
and Karl Marx.

CHAPTER II.

FERDINAND LASSALLE was born of Jewish parents in comfortable circumstances at Breslau in the year 1825, and was educated at the universities of Breslau and Berlin. He became an enthusiastic Hegelian. He wrote articles on it in magazines, had it " on the brain," and preached it " in season and out of season." It is very important for us to notice how men of thought influence men of action. Those who are called practical men often overlook this, and speak as if abstract thinkers exercised no real power over human events. No greater mistake could be made. It is likely that no one of the men whom we shall find to have been powers in the socialistic movement exerted on that movement more vital influence than the German philosopher, who never sat in a legislative chamber, and never addressed a public meeting in his life. We shall find that not only Lassalle, the originator of social democracy in Germany, but Karl Marx, the founder of scientific Socialism, and Bakunin, the apostle of Russian anarchism, drank in eagerly the Hegelian philosophy.

George William Frederick Hegel was born at Stuttgart in 1770, and died of cholera in Berlin in his sixty-first year,

2

when Lassalle was six years old. He received a good
classical education in Würtemberg, and went to Tübingen
to study theology. His sermons were failures; however,
he got a theological certificate, which declared that he
was of " good abilities, middling industry, and especially
deficient in philosophy." Whilst he had not a brilliant
university career, he gathered immense stores of mis-
cellaneous knowledge, and made himself at home in the
Greek and Roman world.

Hunger impelled him to become a private tutor; but
on the death of his father in 1801, he got a small property
that enabled him to relinquish his tutorship, when he
removed to Jena.   There he published his dissertation *De
Orbitis Planetarum*.   In it Newton was treated with scorn
as an empiric.   He ridicules Newton's device, " Physics
beware of metaphysics," by saying it might be translated
" Science beware of thought," and remarks that this precept
the followers of Newton have faithfully followed.

Hegel always treated with contempt those who trust to
facts, rather than to ideas evolved from their own consciousness.   It is interesting to note that, whilst in this
dissertation he satisfactorily proves that there cannot be
a planet between Mars and Jupiter, before the ink was
dry Professor Piazzi had discovered the first of the asteroids,
thus showing how specious and how false an argument
may be when not based on discovered fact, how much
safer it is to trust ourselves to inductive rather than to
deductive logic.

He became *privat-docent* at the University of Jena.
Here his work was brought to an abrupt conclusion by the
battle of Jena.   Like Archimedes at the siege of Syracuse,

he was so engrossed in his work that he continued writing his *Phänomenologie des Geistes*, undisturbed by the thunder of the artillery. Next morning French soldiers made him understand that he would have to give up writing books for a time—at least at Jena. How he viewed the public movements then in progress may be gathered from the close of his lectures on the phenomenology of the mind.

" This, gentlemen, is speculative philosophy as far as I have worked it out. We stand in a momentous time—a seething mass, in which the mind has made a sudden bound, left its old shape behind and is gaining a new. The whole bulk of our old ideas, the very bands of the world, are rent asunder, and collapse like a dream. Mind is preparing a new start. Philosophy, above all things, has to own and welcome such a start. While some in powerless resistance cling to the past, and the majority help, but unconsciously, to swell the numbers of its *cortége*, philosophy, recognising it as the eternal, has to show it due honour."

After various fortunes, teaching school, editing a newspaper, and getting happily married, he was called to a professor's chair in Heidelberg, and in two years after to one in Berlin, where he lectured for thirteen years, formed a school, produced his best works, and made many friends.

This professor, with his old-fashioned face without life or lustre, with a marvellous appetite for snuff, and so bad a delivery that every sentence, and almost every word, seemed to come out with a struggle, influenced in no ordinary degree the men who made Socialism.

We may very well ask, What was his philosophy ? It

is not easy to give a summary of the teaching of eighteen large volumes in a paragraph or two. Especially is this the case with Hegel, for perhaps there is no great writer whose works are more difficult to understand. Scarcely two commentators are agreed as to what he meant to teach. To add to the difficulty of understanding an obscure style, he uses words in different senses.

Every one knows the legend which represents him as saying, " Only one of my pupils understood me," and then adding with a sigh, " and even he misunderstood me." But amongst all that is uncertain or ambiguous in his teaching, it is at any rate certain that he taught the doctrine of evolution. " That the absolute contains within itself, by the very necessity of its nature, a principle of evolution from difference to difference, which differences are its moments." " In the development of humanity we are told by Hegel that the races are moments. The negro race is the natural mind in itself; the Mongolian shows the mind conscious of its opposition to this natural form, and tending to rise above it; the Caucasian is the free mind—mind returned to the absolute unity in itself."

He shows in various ways the value of organization. He teaches distinctly the supremacy of philosophy over revelation. This has led one section of his followers to rank, materialistic atheism. Mr. Lewes in his valuable *History of Philosophy* says: " Remark also that this absolute idealism is Hume's scepticism in dogmatical form. Hume denied the existence of mind and matter, and said there was nothing but ideas. Hegel in effect denies the existence of both object and subject, since the only reality of either depends on its relation to the other."

He also taught the reality of necessary thoughts, a doctrine embodied in his well-known saying: " Whatever is rational is real, whatever is real is rational." Much of his teaching is expressed in the formula: " Thesis, antithesis, synthesis."

After this brief reference to the great teacher of absolute idealism, we return to Lassalle, his ardent disciple. After the dissolution of the first Prussian National Assembly in 1848, a constitution by royal decree was given to that country. This increased the discontent, and added to it the bitterness of disappointment, because the constitution was so much less liberal than had been hoped for by the people. A widespread agitation resulted, and a combination was formed to refuse to pay taxes until popular measures were conceded. At Düsseldorf, Lassalle planned an armed insurrection. The government immediately put the town under a state of siege, and imprisoned Lassalle.

At his trial he claimed the right of active resistance to the decrees of the State when they were not in accordance with the popular will, and condemned the policy of passive resistance.

" Passive resistance," he said, " is a contradiction in itself. It is like Lichtenberg's knife, with blade and without handle, or like the fleece which one must wash without wetting. It is mere inward ill-will without the outward deed. The Crown confiscates the people's freedom, and the Prussian National Assembly, for the people's protection, declares ill-will; it would be unintelligible how the commonest logic should have allowed a legislative assembly to cover itself with such incomparable ridicule, if it were not too intelligible."

He declared himself a "socialist Democrat," and asserted that he was revolutionary on principle. "Revolution," he says, "means merely transformation, and is accomplished when an entirely new principle is—either with force or without it—put in the place of an existing state of things. Reform, on the other hand, is when the principle of the existing state of things is continued, and only developed to more logical or just consequences. The means do not signify. A reform may be carried out by bloodshed, and a revolution in the profoundest tranquillity. The Peasants' War was an attempt to introduce reform by arms, the invention of the spinning-jenny wrought a peaceful revolution."

He had intended to qualify himself as a *privat-docent* at the University of Berlin; but instead of doing so, he devoted himself romantically, and with untiring energy, to the task of redressing the wrongs of the Countess Hatzfeldt. This lady was early married to an unsympathetic husband, a cruel and licentious man, who first neglected and then persecuted her.

Lassalle brought her case before thirty-six different courts, and succeeded in getting a divorce for her, after eight years of toil, in 1851, and then a large fortune in 1854, out of which she settled a considerable sum upon him, that produced an annual income of four thousand thalers, equal to about six hundred pounds. Till Lassalle's death she continued his warmest friend, and after his death was his most sincere mourner.

In showing how he was led to champion her cause, he says: "Her family were silent, but it is said when men keep silent the stones will speak. When every human right is

violated, when even the voice of blood is mute, and help-
less man is forsaken by his born protectors, there then
rises with right man's first and last relation—man. You
have all read with emotion the monstrous history of the
unhappy Duchess of Praslin. Who is there among you
that would not have gone to the death to defend her?
Well, gentlemen, I said to myself, here is Praslin ten
times over. What is the sharp death-agony of an hour
compared with the pangs of death protracted over twenty
years? What are the wounds a knife inflicts compared
with the slow murder dispensed with refined cruelty
throughout a being's whole existence? What are they
compared with the immense woe of this woman, every
right of whose life has been trampled under foot, day
after day, for twenty years, and whom they have first tried
to cover with contempt, that they might then the more
securely overwhelm her with punishment? The difficulties, the sacrifices, the dangers did not deter me. I
determined to meet false appearances with the truth, to
meet rank with right, to meet the power of money with
the power of mind. But if I had known what infamous
calumnies I should have to encounter, how people turned
the purest motives into their contraries, and what ready
credence they gave to the most wretched lies—well, I
hope my purpose would not have been changed, but it
would have cost me a severe and bitter struggle."

These trials brought Lassalle into public notice, and
his boldness, eloquence, and ability, as well as his popular
sympathies, soon made him a powerful influence in the
formation of public opinion.

He was, however, forbidden to enter Berlin. This he

felt as a great privation, as he believed that he could there best serve the cause he had at heart. Accordingly, one day in 1859, he entered it disguised as a wagoner, and, through the mediation of Alexander von Humboldt with the king, was permitted to remain.

In 1862, which we may regard as the beginning of the period of his social activity, he delivered a lecture to a working men's society in Berlin on "The Connexion between the present Epoch of History and the Idea of the Working Class." It was published in the following year. It states that there are three successive stages of evolution in modern history. First, the Feudal Period, when power was in the hands of the landowners, and was used for their benefit. Second, the Bourgeois Period, 1789–1848, when exclusive privileges were taken away from the nobles; power was held by landowners and the *bourgeois*, and was used by them to promote their own interests. Third, the Age of the Working Class; this period commenced in 1848, is not yet established, but is rapidly developing.

"What is the State?" asks Lassalle. "You are the State," he replies. "You are ninety-six per cent. of the population. All political power ought to be of you and through you and for you, and your good and amelioration ought to be the aim of the State. It ought to be so, because your good is not a class interest, but is the national interest."

He teaches that every man has a right to an existence worthy of his moral destiny, and that it is the duty of the State to secure that existence for him; that as no man should be enslaved, as no man should be ignorant, so no

man should be without property, as without property he
cannot enjoy his freedom or his education.

In his *Herr Bastiat-Schulze* he says : " The world is
now face to face with a new social question, the question
whether, since there is no longer any property in the
immediate use of another man, there should still exist
property in his mediate exploitation : *i.e.* whether the free
realization and development of one's power and labour
should be the exclusive private property of the owner of
the instruments and advances necessary for labour—*i.e.* of
capital ; and whether the employer as such, and apart from
the remuneration of his own intellectual labour of management, should be permitted to have property in the value
of other people's labour—*i.e.* whether he ought to receive
what is known as the premium or profit of capital, consisting of the difference between the selling price of the
product and the sum of the wages and salaries of all
kinds of labour, manual and mental, that have contributed
to its production."

He maintains that all instruments of production should
be taken out of private hands and held collectively, as
well as all its products ; that the property of the future
made by the working classes should belong to the working
classes, and that industry should be conducted on the
mutual instead of the proprietary principle.

He unsparingly condemns the present system as being
unjust to the labourer, who can never make more than a
bare subsistence.   " The back of the labourer," he says, " is
the green table on which undertakers and speculators play
the game of fortune which production has become.   It is
the green table on which they receive the heaps of money

thrown to them by the lucky *coup* of the roulette, and which
they smite as they console themselves for an unlucky throw
with the hope of better chances soon. The labourer it is
who pays, with diminished work, with hard-earned savings,
with entire loss of employment, and thus of the means of
subsistence, for the failures entailed in this gambling of
employers and speculators, whose false speculations and
reckonings he has not caused, of whose greed he is not
guilty, and whose good fortune he does not share."

" How is it the workman is so badly off when there is
abundance all around ?   Because of the 'iron economic
law of wages,' according to which the average wages of
labour always remain reduced to the subsistence necessary,
conformably with a nation's standard of life, to the prolongation of existence, and to the propagation of the
species."

" What," asked Lassalle once of a meeting of working
men,—" what is the result of this law, which is unanimously
acknowledged by men of science ?   Perhaps you believe
that you are men ?   But economically considered you are
only commodities.   You are increased by higher wages
like stockings, when there is a lack ; and you are again
got rid of, you are, by means of lower wages—by what
Malthus, the English economist, calls preventive and
destructive checks—decreased like vermin, against which
society wages war."

Contrasting the seller of labour, the working man, with
the seller of other commodities, he points out that while
the merchant, if he cannot get a fair price for his goods,
can reserve them, the workman must sell his labour or
starve.

Lassalle asserts that the State should take the workman out of this wretched condition, and therefore advocates that capital, and land, and means of communication, and banks, should be in the hands of the State. Lassalle was a national and not an international socialist, and believed that each State should settle its own social question for itself. He was also willing to try the formation of " productive associations," which, aided by the State, should gradually exploit the undertaker and the capitalist. Socialists however, as a whole, have not followed him in these two last-mentioned views. They seek for an international, not a national Socialism, and they desire an immediate rather than a gradual change.

He devoted himself with indomitable energy to the diffusion of those opinions. Having an open rupture with the Progressists, who were, whilst professedly Liberals, not sufficiently democratic for Lassalle, he wrote his open letter, which has been called the charter of German Socialism, drew up a working man's programme, and wrote his *Herr Bastiat - Schulze*, his largest economic work. Schulze was a leading member of the Progressist party, and Bastiat was the populariser in France of the orthodox political economy. Lassalle accused Schulze of being merely the echo of Bastiat, and therefore calls him "Bastiat-Schulze." The work is full of gross personalities, but presents some of Lassalle's views with much clearness and vigour. He spoke with great force, and often turned a hostile audience into a friendly and sympathetic one. The working men forsook Schulze and the Progressist party, and on May 23, 1863, Lassalle founded the " Universal German Working Men's Association " at Leipsic. He was

elected president for five years, and in July, 1864, he had
enrolled over four thousand members.

Lassalle, although the champion of the poor, and working with such energy, was of fashionable and luxurious
habits. He was a connoisseur of wines. His suppers
were exquisite entertainments. He liked to surround himself with what was rare in art and gay in society. His
friend Heine, recognising his acuteness and power of
expression and practical ability, at the same time says,
" He is a genuine son of the new era, without even the
pretence of modesty or self-denial, who will assert and
enjoy himself in the world of realities." In some fashionable circle he met a young lady, Helena von Dönnigsen,
accomplished and clever, but somewhat eccentric, and, like
Lassalle himself, not at all disposed to be fettered by the
conventionalities of society. After his severe labours,
Lassalle went to Switzerland for much-needed rest, and
again he met this young lady. He was most anxious to
marry her; she was even more than willing. But her father,
a German diplomatist, was decidedly opposed to it; so
were all her friends, whose sympathies and interests were
bound up with the court party. At last, yielding to their
persuasions, she gave up Lassalle and consented to marry
Herr von Racowitza.

Lassalle sent a challenge to both father and bridegroom.
The latter accepted it, and in the duel Lassalle was fatally
wounded. A little less passion and vanity, and a little
more saving common-sense and self-control, and he might
have lived for many years. He died August 31, 1864, at
the age of thirty-nine.

Many demonstrations were made as the body was taken

to Germany. His death caused much lamentation and woe. The mourners went about the streets. He was gathered to his fathers, and his remains repose in the Jewish burying-ground of his native place. Over his grave is the inscription : " Lassalle—Thinker and Fighter."

What, we may ask, was Lassalle's contribution to Socialism ? It is quite true that his plan of productive association with State credit has not been a practical success, whilst the co-operative societies founded by his great antagonist Schulze have proved to be an admirable means of improving the condition, and of giving valuable training to the working man. They have been contrasted as Self - help *versus* State - help. Yet Lassalle first led the Socialists to organize themselves as a distinct party, and made clear the fundamental difference between them and the Progressists in their idea of the functions of the State. According to the Progressists, the State was to be a " night watchman to prevent robbery and burglary." According to Lassalle, the State is to help in every way in procuring the development, culture, and happiness of the individual. Lassalle's statement of the " iron law of wages," by which far too small a portion of the produce of labour goes to the labourer, was his chief and special point in the economics of Socialism. This he endeavoured, with much force of reasoning and variety of illustration, to impress on his followers, and succeeded in convincing them that nothing less than an entire revolution in the existing industrial arrangements would give the worker that share of the means of enjoyment to which he is equitably entitled. This matter we shall consider further in another part of this lecture.

CHAPTER III.

WE have now to consider another and in many respects
a greater name. The man who has done more to make
Socialism what it is to-day than Lassalle, or any one else,
is Karl Marx. If Lassalle was the orator of Socialism,
Marx was its philosopher. Karl Marx is called the "Father
of scientific Socialism," and his great work on *Capital* is
called the "Socialists' Bible." As a student and thinker,
as an organizer and "man of affairs," he must be placed in
a high rank amongst the men who have made history in
the nineteenth century. Like Lassalle and many men of
mark, he was of Jewish blood, both his parents being of
that race.

He was born at Trèves,—famous for its holy coat,—in
the Rhine Provinces, on May 5, 1818. Originally the
name of the family was Mordecai—a name that suggests to
us unwavering devotion to the Hebrew God, the luxurious
Persian court, and the haughty Haman, who digged a pit
for another and fell into it himself. Karl's grandfather
changed the name to Marx.

When Trèves fell into the hands of Prussia, it is said
that the father of Karl Marx was offered the choice of

either renouncing his religion, or of giving up his profession as an advocate. He renounced Judaism, gained the favour of the Prussians, and obtained a good appointment under the government. It is possible that this incident may account for the bitterness with which Marx attacks Christianity, for it is certain that a religion thus forced by unworthy motives would raise a prejudice against itself on the part of every fair and candid mind.

Marx studied at Bonn, and Jena, and at Berlin; philosophy, political economy, and particularly history, attracted his attention. At the university he became, like Lassalle, an ardent Hegelian ; and this system of philosophy affected his mode of thought and of expression throughout his entire after life.

He was urged by his friends to adopt an academic career, and his marriage with the sister of Von Westfalen, a Prussian minister of state, would have helped in that sphere; but just as he had finished his college course Friedrich Wilhelm IV. (1840) began to reign.

The Liberals of Germany thought that a new era would commence with the new king, that the day of liberty had dawned at last. In order to take an active part in promoting the reforms that were supposed to be at hand, Marx turned his attention to journalism, and joined the staff of the *Rhenish Gazette*, the organ of the "Young Hegelian" or "Philosophical Radical Party." The ability he displayed soon caused him to be appointed editor. His attacks on the government were so vigorous and telling, that a special censor was sent from Berlin to Cologne, and ultimately the journal was suppressed by the Prussian government in 1843. He then went to Paris, continued his connexion with journalism, and met many men who were amongst the moving spirits of that day—some of whom have left permanent names in literature and social philosophy. By his intercourse with them Marx was modified, moulded, and developed, as might be expected; for a number of vigorous thinkers frequently meeting and freely discussing the burning questions of a time exceptionally full of such questions, could not but act and react upon each other to their mutual intellectual advantage.

These friends of Marx are noteworthy.

Arnold Ruje, a Nationalist rather than a Socialist, was involved continually in revolutionary movements, and at the early age of twenty-two was sentenced to five years' imprisonment. After taking part in the disturbances of 1848 he came to England, where he stayed till his death. He has written largely, poetry and philosophy as well as politics and fiction.

Heinrich Heine was an extreme Democrat rather than a Socialist. On account of the virulence of his writings he had to leave Germany in 1831, and went to Paris, where he died some quarter of a century later.

Michael Bakunin, a born revolutionist, belonged to a rich and noble Russian family. He was twice sentenced to death. He was imprisoned by the Prussian, the Austrian, and the Russian governments. He escaped from East Siberia, visited far Japan, and came back to Europe to plunge again into a very whirlpool of revolutionary movements. With Bakunin we shall meet again, more than once.

Ludwig Andreas Feuerbach must receive a more extended notice. He was born in 1804. He went to Heidelberg as a theological student, and, like Lassalle and Marx, became a Hegelian. He was appointed a professor, but resigned his chair on account of his views on the immortality of the soul. He transformed the pure idealism of Hegel into humanism, and it was mainly through this humanism that the young Hegelians became Socialists. This philosopher exercised an influence on Socialism second only to that of Hegel himself.

We have seen something of what Hegel taught. Feuerbach sought to abolish the transcendency of reason. Following the Positivist order of thought, he says : "God was my first thought, reason my second, man my third and last." He gave up theology, then he gave up metaphysics, and finally adopted a system of pure materialism. He regards the body as the totality and essence of man's being. Therefore man's enjoyment and welfare in his present life, which will be his only one, should be the supreme object of desire and effort, the sole object aimed at by religious, political, or social organizations. "Man," he says, "man alone is our god, our father, our judge, our redeemer, our true home, our law and rule, the alpha and omega of our political, moral, public, and domestic life and work. There is no salvation but by man." He teaches that human nature, with all its appetites and passions, is holy, that all gratifications of desire are right, that every man ought to be happy, that all should help each, and that each should help all in the attainment of it. The practical side of this teaching is democratic Socialism. There is an analogy between politics and religion. In religion we have God a spiritual King, and men subjects in the kingdom of God. In the State we have a temporal king, and men the subjects of that monarch. Both God and king must be abolished.

The State must be humanized.   The sovereign people must be both king and god.

"The princes are gods," says Feuerbach, "and they must share the same fate.   The dissolution of theology into anthropology in the field of thought is the dissolution of monarchy into republic in the field of politics.   Dualism, separation is the essence of theology ; dualism, separation is the essence of monarchy.   There we have the antithesis of God and world ; here we have the antithesis of State and people."

Feuerbach's peculiar ethical principle has been called "tuism" to distinguish it from "egoism."   "The nature of man," he says, "is contained only in the community, in the union of man with man.   Isolation is finitude and limitation, community is freedom and infinity.   Man by himself is but man ; man with man, the unity of I and Thou, is god."   The humanists, thus regarding the social man as the true unit, were opponents of the individualistic basis of society, and friends of its socialistic reconstruction.   Thus through humanism Hegelians became Socialists.

There were, however, in many points considerable divergences of opinion.   When they endeavoured to forecast the future social State, they differed.   They could agree to pull down the present social system, but they could not agree as to what they would build up in its place.   Therefore they gave themselves up to the work that divided them least.

Marr, a humanist, says in his book on *Secret Societies in Switzerland :* "The masses can only be gathered under the flag of negation.   When you present detailed plans, you excite controversies and sow divisions ; you repeat the mistake of the French Socialists, who have scattered their redoubtable forces, because they tried to carry formulated systems. We are content to lay down the foundation of the revolution. We shall have deserved well of it, if we stir hatred and contempt against all existing institutions. We make war against all prevailing ideas of religion, of the State, of country, of patriotism. The idea of God is the keystone of a perverted civilization. It must be destroyed. The true root of liberty, of equality, of culture, is atheism. Nothing must restrain the spontaneity of the human mind."

Marx advanced with Feuerbach and became a humanist. He regarded humanism as the ferment that would leaven the social State of the future. " The new revolution," he says, " will be introduced by philosophy. The revolutionary tradition of Germany is theological. The Reformation was the work of a monk; the revolution will be the work of a philosopher."

In the view of Marx it was the highest duty to destroy everything in the present order of things that makes man a degraded, insulted, forsaken, and despised being. In order to carry this out, the proletariat must unite and act. They have been oppressed and trampled upon. They are without property. They have been defrauded. In order that they may enjoy life and possess power, they must possess property. Private property must therefore cease.

" The only practical emancipation for Germany is an emancipation proceeding from the standpoint of the theory which explains man to be the highest being for man. In Germany the emancipation from the Middle Ages is only possible, as at the same time an emancipation from the partial conquests of the Middle Ages. In Germany one

kind of bond cannot be broken without all other bonds
being broken too.   Germany is by nature too thorough
to be able to revolutionise without revolutionising from a
fundamental principle, and following that principle to its
utmost limits; and therefore the emancipation of Germany
will be the emancipation of man.   The head of this
emancipation is philosophy, its heart is the proletariat."

In Paris, Marx also met *Friedrich Engels*, the most
intimate and trusted of all his companions, his "lifelong
and loyal friend and companion in arms."   Whilst Marx
was often engaged in conflicts with those of his own party,
or those who were nearly allied to his own party,—for in
Socialism, as in other systems, we see that "it is not the
colours that hate each other, but the shades," and in
Socialism there are many shades,—there was never any
difference or coolness between Marx and Engels.   They
were faithful to each other through good and bad report,
through good and evil fortune.   Amongst men prone to
suspicion and afflicted with that rottenness of the bones,
envy,—according to John Stuart Mill, the most anti-social
of all the vices,—neither envy nor suspicion ever marred
their friendship.   Marx, the philosophical journalist, and
Engels, the veteran Communist, worked together as if they
had entered into a solemn league and covenant.

On account of Marx's continued attacks in the press on
the Prussian government, he was expelled from Paris in
1845, and settled at Brussels.   There he wrote the *Misery
of Philosophy*, as an answer to Proudhon's *Philosophy of
Misery*, a proceeding which caused a final breach between
the two authors.   He also published a merciless criticism
on the medley of French-English Socialism and Com-

munism and German philosophy which then constituted
the secret doctrine of the Communist League, and insisted
that their work could have no tenable theoretical basis,
except that of a scientific insight into the economic structure of society, and that this ought to be put in a popular
form, not with the view of carrying out every utopian
system, but of promoting among the working and other
classes a self-conscious participation in the process of the
historical transformation of society that was taking place
under their eyes.

In order to carry this out, there ought to be a public
and vigorous propaganda of socialist principles, and a
wisely directed effort to educate public opinion in their
views. The strictures of Marx were well taken. A
congress was held in London, where a society of Socialists,
chiefly composed of German immigrants, had been established. Marx and Engels were invited to be present,
and to draw up a " Manifesto of the Communist Party."
This was done in 1848. It became the creed of the
International Socialists, and greatly enhanced the reputation of the two friends. Instead of the old watchword,
" All men are brothers," it adopts a new one, " Proletarians
of all countries, unite ! "

The changes occurring in society are set forth in it;
the decay of feudalism, the supremacy of the *bourgeoisie*,
the condition of the proletariat, by far the largest section
of society, kept in poverty, without property or power or
anything worth calling a home. It demands a republic,
the payment of members of Parliament, the conversion of
large estates, mines, etc., into State property, the appropriation by the State of all means of transport, such as

railways, canals, steamships, roads, and ports, the restriction of the law of succession, the introduction of a heavily graded income tax, the abolition of indirect taxation by abolishing excise duties, the establishment of national workshops, State guarantee to all work-people of an existence, and a provision for the incapable, universal and free education. As to the means of bringing all these changes about, the proletariat must gain political power, and possession of all property must be in the hands of the State.

The manifesto may be summed up as demanding—

(1) Expropriation of landed property, and application of rent to State expenditure; (2) Abolition of inheritance; (3) Confiscation of the property of all emigrants and rebels; (4) Centralization of credit in the hands of the State by means of a national bank, with State capital and exclusive monopoly; (5) Centralization of all means of transport in hands of State; (6) Institution of national factories, and improvement of lands on a common plan; (7) Compulsory obligation of labour upon all equally, and establishment of industrial armies, especially for agriculture; (8) Joint prosecution of agriculture and mechanical arts, and gradual abolition of the distinction of town and country; (9) Public and gratuitous education for all children, abolition of children's labour in factories, etc. The manifesto ends by saying: "The Communists do not seek to conceal their views and aims. They declare openly that their purpose can only be obtained by a violent overthrow of all existing arrangements of society. Let the ruling classes tremble at a communistic revolution. The proletariat have nothing to lose in it but their

chains; they have a world to win. Proletarians of all
countries, unite!"

During the revolution of 1848, Marx was expelled
from Brussels, and went by invitation of the provisional
government to Paris. After a few weeks, when the
German revolution broke out, he went to Cologne, and
there, with Engels and others, started the *New Rhenish
Gazette.* This journal urged the people to stop paying
taxes till the desired reforms were effected. It was
suppressed by the government after the Dresden insurrection was quelled. Its last number appeared in red type
in June, 1849, and contained Freilegrath's *Farewell of the
" New Rhenish Gazette":*

> Farewell, but not for ever farewell!
>   They cannot kill the spirit, my brother;
> In thunder I'll rise on the field where I fell,
>   More boldly to fight out another.
> When the last of crowns, like glass, shall break
>   On the scene our sorrows have haunted,
> And the people its last dread "Guilty" shall speak, .
>   By your side you shall find me undaunted.
> On Rhine or on Danube, in war and deed,
>   You shall witness, true to his vow,
> On the wrecks of thrones, in the midst of the field,
>   The rebel who greets you now.

After this Marx went to London, and devoted himself
to the study of economic questions, matured his views on
capital, was a constant reader in the British Museum
library, was correspondent for the *New York Tribune,* and
produced several pamphlets, one against Louis Napoleon,
another against Lord Palmerston, and another against a
fellow Socialist, Karl Vogt.

In 1864, Marx returned from his comparative retirement, and once more took an active and conspicuous part in public affairs. Two years before, there had been the International Exhibition of London, to which a deputation of working-men came from France. They were entertained by some English working-men at the Freemasons' Tavern. Their ideas regarding the identity of the interests of labour, and the importance of united action for promoting them, were interchanged. In the following year another deputation arrived, and the same subjects were discussed; and then, in 1864, a public meeting of working-men of different nationalities was held in St. Martin's Hall, London. A committee of fifty was appointed, about one-half of them English, and commissioned to draw up a constitution of the new association; and thus was founded the most important, influential, and at one time most dreaded of all socialistic associations, "The International Working-men's Association."

Mazzini was connected with it at first. He, however, was too moderate; and as there was not much cordiality between him and Marx, he soon retired from it, and ever after used his influence against it.

Again Marx, who was the dominant influence and practical founder of the association, urged as the watch-word, "Proletarians of all countries, unite!" It was declared that the economic subjection of the labourer to the possessor of the means of labour, *i.e.* of the sources of life, is the first cause of his political, moral, and material servitude, and that the economic emancipation of labour is consequently the great aim to which every political movement ought to be subordinated.

The International continued to be a revolutionary force,

and a name of dread, until the establishment of the Paris Commune, after the outbreak of the Franco-German war. If the leaders of the International did not actively promote the Commune, it is certain that they heartily approved of and deeply sympathised with it. Marx made no secret of his views on the subject. But its excesses led the English members to forsake the International, and at the congress at the Hague in 1872 it was divided into two strongly antagonistic parties.

One party was the Centralist Democratic Socialists, under the leadership of Marx ; and the other was the Anarchist Socialists, under the leadership of Michael Bakunin. The difference between these parties was of an exceedingly serious character.

The Centralist Democratic Socialists maintained that, under the scheme of collective property, co-operative production would only be possible under one great central authority, armed with sufficient power to enforce its decisions.

The Anarchist Socialists adopted the principle of Proudhon,—as we have seen, an old opponent of Marx, —that the true form of the State is anarchy : meaning by that, not disorder, but the absence of any supreme authority, either king, parliament, or convention, the absence of all control, and the management of property and all industrial enterprises by groups of working-men voluntarily associating themselves together.

After the fall of the International, Marx ceased to take an active part in public affairs, but devoted himself to the completion of his great work, *Das Kapital*, till his death, in Paris, in the spring of 1883.

His work on *Capital* consists of two large volumes. The first volume, published in 1867, treats of the "Production of Capital"; and the second, published in 1885, treats of its circulation. This work shows immense research, no fewer than three hundred and fifty English authors being quoted in it. It is characterized by keen analysis, and by a patient and profound investigation of the subject. It is spoken of by Socialists in terms of rapturous approval.

Dr. Aveling says of it: "That which Darwin did for biology, Marx has done for economics. Each of them by long and patient observation, experiment, recordal, reflection, arrived at an immense generalization,—a generalization the like of which their particular branch of science had never seen; a generalization that not only revolutionised that branch, but is actually revolutionising the whole of human thought, the whole of human life. And that the generalization of Darwin is at present much more universally accepted than that of Marx, is probably due to the fact that the former affects our intellectual rather than our economic life—can, in a word, be accepted in a measure alike by the believers in the capitalistic system and by its opponents. There can be little doubt that the two names by which the nineteenth century will be known, as far as its thinking is concerned, will be those of Charles Darwin and Karl Marx."

Marx distinguishes between *utility* value and *exchange* value. Thus atmospheric air has great utility value, but no exchange value. On the other hand, a diamond has little utility value, but great exchange value. The difference is caused by labour: nothing in which labour is

not solidified has exchange value. If there was no labour
in getting diamonds, they would have no exchange value.
The value is the labour materialised in any article.

He says: "As values in exchange all commodities are
only definite masses of congested labour time," and "that
a day's labour of given length always turns out a product
of the same value."

He endeavours to show that capital cannot be made
by the exchange of commodities. "Considered abstractly,
or independently of circumstances which do not proceed
from the inherent laws of the simple circulation of
commodities, the act of exchange is, apart from the
substitution of one use-value by another, merely a metamorphosis, a change of form in the commodities. The
same value—that is, the same quantity of incorporated
social labour — remains in the hand of each owner of
the commodity: first, in the form of his commodity;
then in the form of money which it has assumed;
and, finally, of the commodity to which the money is
again changed. This change of form does not imply
a change in the magnitude of the value. But the
change which the value of the commodity itself undergoes
in this process is confined to a change of its money-form.
This form exists, first, as the price of the commodity
offered for sale; then as a sum of money,—expressed,
however, in the price already; and, finally, as the price
of an equivalent commodity. This change of form *per se*
as little implies a change in the magnitude of the value
as does the exchange of a five-pound note for sovereigns,
half-sovereigns, and shillings. Thus, so far as the circulation of the commodity only implies a change in the form

of its value, it implies, when the phenomenon takes place in a pure form, the exchange of equivalents."

" The formation of surplus value, and therefore the conversion of money into capital, can thus be explained neither by the assumption that the sellers dispose of their commodities above their value, nor that the buyers purchase them below their value."

Capital thus not arising from any of the processes. of exchange, whence then does it arise ? Marx shows, or at least aims at showing, that it results from the exploitation of the labourer by the capitalist.

Labour, like every other commodity, has a utility value and an exchange value. The labourer does not get his utility value for his work, but only its exchange value, which is by the iron and necessary law of wages what will suffice to keep him; and the race of labourers and the difference between this and his utility value is taken by the capitalist. The labourer cannot insist on getting his utility value, because he must sell his labour or starve.

Labour may be divided into *socially necessary* labour and *surplus* labour.

Socially necessary labour is that which is necessary to keep the labourer, according to the ideas of what is necessary in his age and place. Suppose a labourer by working four hours can make what is necessary to keep him, then, if he works ten hours, four hours are socially necessary labour, and six hours are surplus labour. Again, suppose that a man working ten hours at a piece of leather, worth eight shillings, can make it, as shoes, worth eighteen shillings, and that he gets for his labour four shillings : there is thus created for the capitalist six shillings, the value of the surplus labour of the labourer.

Capital is thus created entirely by the labourer working for a longer time than he need work, in order to keep himself and to keep up a supply of labourers. It is therefore the constant aim of the capitalist to keep wages low and the hours of labour long, so that his capital may grow with ever-increasing velocity. Consequently there can be no peace between labour and capital.

" There is now," says Marx, " to be expropriated, not the independently working labourer, but the capitalist exploiting many labourers. This expropriation is effected by the working of the immanent laws of this very capitalist production, by the centralization of capital. One capitalist ever kills many. Hand in hand with this centralization, or the expropriation of many capitalists by few, are developed the co-operative form of the labour process,— and that on a constantly increasing scale,—the intelligent application of science to technical purposes, the systematic exploitation of the soil, the transformation of the means of labour into means of labour only usable in common, the economising of all means of production by their use for production by combined social labour, the entwining of all nations in the net of the world-market, and thus the international character of the capitalist *régime.* With the steady decrease of the capital magnates, who usurp and monopolise all the advantages of this process of transformation, the mass of want, oppression, servitude, degradation, and spoliation grows ; but the revolt of the labouring class —swelling ever in numbers, and disciplined, united, and organized by the mechanism of the capitalist process of

production itself—spreads at the same time.   The capitalist
monopoly becomes a fetter on the mode of production with
and under which it has originated.   The centralization of
the means of production and the socialization of labour
reach a point at which they become no longer compatible
with their capitalist integument, and this is burst asunder.
The last hour of capitalist private property strikes.   The
expropriators are expropriated."

This expropriation of the expropriators is to be accomplished by any means, at any cost.   He further says :

"It cannot be said that the social movement excludes
the political.   There is no political movement that is not
at the same time social.   Only by so ordering things that
there shall be no classes and no class distinctions, will
social evolutions cease to be political revolutions.   Until
then, on the eve of every general reorganization of society
the final word of social science will always run, ' Combat
or death, bloody war or nothing.'   There is the question
inexorably put."

Marx contends that industrial improvements—the use of
machinery and of labour-saving apparatus—are all against
the labourer and in favour of the capitalist.   Machinery
enables more work to be done with less expenditure of
human labour, and so enables one man to do the work of
ten, which is equivalent to making him work so much
longer, and consequently there is so much more surplus
labour for the capitalist.

Machinery involving largely the work of mere superintendence, as in weaving factories, enables the cheaper
work of women and children to be used, so that the
capitalist can get the labour of an entire family for what

ought to be the value of the labour of the head of the household.

Machinery can go on for ever; and the tendency of using it will always be to make those who have spent capital in acquiring it take more and more out of the labourer in order to make him keep pace with the machinery.

The contribution of Marx to Socialism was very great. The chief part, not by any means the entire of it, was his exposition of capital. In this he gives a scientific justification of the discontent of the labourer and of the demands of the Socialist. He endeavoured to show, with greater wealth of learning and greater power of analysis than Rodbertus or any other writer, that all capital was made by labour, and should belong to the labourers. His teaching on this subject is the orthodox doctrine of Socialists to-day, and is indeed the only legitimate justification of their economic ideas. Those ideas are built on the doctrines of Marx. In another part of this lecture we hope to show the absolute falseness of his doctrines; and when the foundations are destroyed the superstructure must perish.

In sketching the lives of Lassalle and Marx, the history of Socialism in Germany has been necessarily delineated. It is, however, necessary to notice a very important congress held at Gotha in 1875, at which a programme was adopted that has been substantially the programme of the Democratic Socialists ever since. It consists of two parts, a part for the present and for the future; or, as it has been said, of three parts, the programme for to-day, the programme for to-morrow, and the programme for the day after to-morrow.

THE GOTHA PROGRAMME.

" I. Labour is the source of all wealth and civilization ;
and since productive labour as a whole is made possible
only in and through society, the entire produce of labour
belongs to society : that is, it belongs by an equal right to
all its members, each according to his reasonable needs,
upon condition of a universal obligation to labour.

" In existing society the instruments of labour are the
monopoly of the capitalist class ; the dependence of the
labouring class which results therefrom is the cause of
misery and servitude in all forms.

" The emancipation of labour requires the conversion of
the instruments of labour into the common property of
society, and the management of labour by association, and
the application of the product with a view to the general
good, and an equitable distribution.

" The emancipation of labour must be the work of the
labouring class, in relation to which all other classes are
only a reactionary mass.

" II. Starting from these principles, the Socialistic Labour
Party of Germany seeks by all lawful means to establish
a free State and a socialistic society, to break asunder the
iron law of wages by the abolition of the system of wage-
labour, the suppression of every form of exploitation, and
the correction of all political and social inequality.

" The Socialistic Labour Party of Germany, although at
first working within national limits, is sensible of the
international character of the labour movement, and is
resolved to fulfil all the duties thereby laid on working
men, in order to realize the brotherhood of all men.

"The Socialistic Labour Party of Germany demands, in order to pave the way for the solution of the social question, the establishment by State help of socialistic productive associations under the democratic control of the workpeople. Productive associations for industry and agriculture should be created to such an extent that the socialistic organization of all labour may arise out of them.

"The Socialistic Labour Party of Germany demands as the basis of the State : (1) Universal, equal, and direct suffrage, together with secret and obligatory voting, for all citizens over twenty years of age, in all elections in State and commune. The election day must be a Sunday or holiday. (2) Direct legislation by the people. Decision on peace or war by the people. (3) Universal liability to military service. Militia instead of standing army. (4) Abolition of all exceptional laws, especially laws interfering with liberty of the press, of association, and of meeting ; in general, all laws restricting free expression of opinion, free thought, and free enquiry. (5) Administration of justice by the people. Gratuitous justice. (6) Universal, compulsory, gratuitous, and equal education of the people by the State. Religion to be declared a private affair.

"The Socialistic Labour Party of Germany demands within the conditions of existing society : (1) The utmost possible extension of political rights and liberties in the sense of the above demands. (2) The replacement of all existing taxes, and especially of indirect taxes, which peculiarly burden the people, by a single progressive income tax for State and commune. (3) Unrestricted right of combination. (4) A normal working day corresponding to the needs of society. Prohibition of Sunday

4

labour.   (5) Prohibition of the labour of children, and of
all labour for women that is injurious to health and
morality.   (6) Laws for protection of the life and health
of workmen.   Sanitary control of workmen's dwellings.
Inspection of mines, factories, workshops, and home industry by officers chosen by working-men.   An effective
Employers' Liability Act.   (7) Regulation of prison labour.
(8) Entire freedom of management for all funds for the
assistance and support of working-men."

The phrase " by lawful means " was left out from the first
paragraph of the second part of the Wyden Conference of
1880, in consequence of the anti-socialist laws that were
passed because of the Socialist attempts on the life of the
Emperor William in 1878, and was not reinserted at the
Halle Conference of 1891.

Minor modifications were made, as, for example, asking
for an eight hours' instead of a ten hours' day, thirty-six
hours' continuous and uninterrupted rest, instead of the
Sunday rest; but the changes were so slight that we may
regard the Gotha programme as a full and accurate
expression of the demands of Democratic Socialism.

The violent section in Germany is not sufficiently strong
to form a separate party.   Some of them were expelled
in 1880 and others in 1891, when they urged an earnest
crusade against the Church and religion.   They were
answered by Leibknecht.

"Instead," said he, "of squandering our strength in a
struggle with the Church and sacerdotalism, let us go to
the root of the matter.   We desire to overthrow the State
of the classes.   When we have done that, the Church and

sacerdotalism will fall with it; and in this respect we are much more radical and much more definite in purpose than our opponents, for we like neither the priests nor the anti-priests."

The Democratic Socialists are a powerful party in Germany; at the general election this year 1893 they returned forty-four members to the Reichstag, being an increase of eight over the number returned at the election of 1890. They polled four hundred thousand votes more than the Ultramontanes, who in 1890 ran them very close. They are thus the numerically strongest party in the empire, and during the last three years have increased about twenty-two per cent.

Besides the Democratic Socialists of Germany, there are three modifications of Socialism of sufficient importance to demand our attention.

CHAPTER IV.

Christian Socialism—Saint-Simon—Dr. Döllinger—Ketteler—Moufang —St. Joseph Associations—Pastor Todt—Dr. Stöcker—Socialists of the Chair—State Socialism—Prince Bismarck.

CHRISTIAN SOCIALISM.—There are two developments of Christian Socialism that we must examine, one in Germany and another in England. We shall examine Christian Socialism in Germany now, and defer the examination of Christian Socialism in England, until we consider the development of Socialism in that country.

There was an element of Christian Socialism in the system of Saint-Simon. He was a French noble, and in his last work, *Nouveau Christianisme* (1825), he teaches that the principle of Christian fraternity should lead all classes above the lowest "to labour for the development, material, moral, and intellectual, of the class the most numerous and the poorest." In order that this might be accomplished, he argued that there must be a radical reform of the institution of property and inheritance.

Many connected with the Churches looked on Socialism as being one of those evil things which have in them a "soul of goodness," and believed that, if it could be purged of its atheism and antitheism, materialism and revolutionary elements, it might be made a valuable instrument for the elevation of humanity. They were disposed to accept the theory of value propounded by Marx, and to aid in securing a higher standard of living for the working-man.

Dr. Döllinger, a high authority in the Church of Rome before the dogma of the Papal infallibility had been pronounced, afterwards the head of the Old Catholic movement, recommended the Catholic clubs of Germany to discuss the question, so that a socialism under the guidance and benediction of the Church might prevail.

William Immanuel Baron von Ketteler, Bishop of Mayence, a man of high rank and immense energy, wrote a pamphlet, in which he declared : " It is no longer possible to doubt that the whole material existence of almost the entire labouring population,—*i.e.* of much the greatest part of men in modern States, and of their families,—that the daily question about the necessary bread for man, wife, and children, is exposed to all the fluctuations of the market and of the price of commodities. I know nothing more . deplorable than this fact. What sensations must it cause in those poor men who, with all they hold dear, are day after day at the mercy of the accidents of market price ? That is the slave market of our Liberal Europe, fashioned after the model of our humanist, rationalistic, antichristian Liberalism and freemasonry."

He also advocated that the Church should voluntarily raise a large sum of money to be used for starting productive associations, and that these associations should be both carried on and owned by working-men.

Moufang, another ecclesiastic, is more disposed to lean on the State to aid industrial undertakings than on voluntary contributions, and advocates that the State should protect

the working-man against injurious surroundings—working
too long and for too little remuneration ; also that it ought
to reduce the taxes and military burdens of the working
classes.

Many clubs, called Christian Social Associations, or from
the name of their patron saint, himself a working-man, St.
Joseph Associations, exist to carry out those views. By
their means many hope to preserve the working-men in
the Church of Rome, and to save them from the objectionable principles and practices of the Social Democrats.

More than ten years after the Roman Catholic Christian
socialistic movement began, a similar one was instituted
by Protestants. They thought that, whilst Democratic
Socialists and Roman Catholic Socialists were manifesting
such anxiety to improve the condition of the working-man,
it was neither wise nor becoming for Protestants to appear
indifferent to his interests. Many of them also seem to
have been convinced of the truth of the economic theories
of Marx and Lassalle.

Pastor Rudolph Todt, in his work on *Radical German
Socialism and Christian Society*, maintains that the New
Testament is an authoritative guide on economic questions.
He condemns the present system of capitalistic production,
and maintains that there is a close affinity between Christianity and Socialism, insomuch that "every merely
nominal Christian is a spiritual Manchestrist worshipping
laisser faire with his whole soul, and that a Manchestrist
is never a true Christian."

His analysis of Democratic Socialism is that it consists
of three elements : first, in economics, communism ; second,
in politics, republicanism ; and third, in religion, atheism.

He accepts its first and second elements, communism and republicanism, but regards its third, atheism, as a mistake, and seems inclined to think that, if Socialists adopted Christianity instead of atheism, their triumph would be immediate and complete.

Amongst the Evangelicals who have joined the movement, a foremost place must be allotted to Dr. Stöcker, court preacher at Berlin. At an International Conference of the Evangelical Alliance, held in Florence in 1891, he said: " With the exception of a few narrow-minded believers, we all desire that that which is good in the aims of the social democracy should be accomplished; but no reasonable person approves of the evil objects among them, anarchy, unbelief, annihilation of personal liberty, and the destruction of family life.

"A change in men's thoughts has plainly come about. The Manchester School is no longer followed. The reign of Socialism has begun. Fundamentally it is a Christian law which is reorganized, the royal law of love, which for eighteen centuries all believers have obeyed in thought if not in practice. The Manchester School of political economy has done a good work in its time, especially in the direction of personal liberty and development of human energy and talent in connexion with natural forces, thus giving an immense impulse to economic life; but the principle of it was *individualism*. We see now the insufficiency of it, and all society is filled with the *social* spirit. The abstract humanity of Rousseau, with its idea of individual contract at the root of the State, is gone. The Church which Voltaire attacked with his sarcasm, and Lessing with his rationalism, is no longer a citadel of truth, but a ruin. Economical science in those days had for its motto, ' Laisser faire,' 'laisser aller.' The optimism which came from the school of Leibnitz, and believed that the best of all possible worlds would come out of forces left entirely to themselves, is passed away as a dream. The result of such a development of individual power has been seen to be egoism and mammonism—a materialism which, while it gathered the fruits of men's labour, neglected their personal and family life. Hence the terrible war of classes and interests which has ensued. In Germany, science has renounced the old theories, and the consequence is that they have been abandoned in practice. Economic individualism has proved itself an utter failure."

There are now various organizations under Protestant influences labouring for the elevation of the working classes. These associations differ more or less amongst themselves on the measure of aid to be received from the State, on the extent to which individuals should be permitted to hold private property, and to what extent the property of deceased persons should be taxed. On the whole, however, they accept the practical programme of the Democratic Socialists, divested of its atheistic and revolutionary elements.

These Christian Socialists have not been at all successful in gaining the confidence of the Democratic Socialists, whilst the bulk of the Reformed Churches regard and denounce them, as neither sound interpreters of Holy Scripture, nor loyal to their religious principles.

SOCIALISTS OF THE CHAIR.—The term *Katheder-Social-istens* was first used by Oppenheim in 1872, to designate and ridicule certain professors who to a large extent sympathised with the views and sentiments of Lassalle, yet were opposed to the German free trade or Manchester party, as well as to the Democratic Socialists.

These professors called together a congress at Eisenach in October, 1872, at which were prominent politicians, professors of economic science at the German universities, leaders of working-men, and large capitalists. A number of papers on factory legislation, trades unions, strikes, labourers' dwellings, and cognate subjects were read and amply discussed. At this congress, Professor Schmolle, for himself and his friends, like the disciples at Antioch, accepted the designation first given in contempt, and by it they have since been specifically known.

These Socialists of the Chair belong to the historical school of political economists. This school studies what nations have thought, willed, and discovered in the economic field, what they have striven after, what they have attained to, and by what means and under what conditions they have attained it. They do not confine their attention to a number of contemporaneous facts, but view matters in their historical development. Hence they see how an economic system, at one time good and serviceable, may be unwise and inexpedient at a different stage of social culture. They are opposed to the theory of cosmopolitanism— that is, that there is an economic system equally adapted to every country; and to perpetualism—that is, that there is a system applicable to every social stage.

The Socialists of the Chair insist on the necessity of accentuating the moral element in economic study. They repudiate self-interest as the sole economic force, and point out that other forces—the sense of justice, the obligations of religion, individual and national idiosyn-

crasies, honour, etc.—influence, and ought to influence,
men in the three spheres of activity: (1) private economy;
(2) compulsory public economy; (3) the caritative or
philanthropic sphere.

"There are," says Roscher, "as many different ideals as
there are different types of peoples." He casts aside the
notion generally received before his time, that there is a
single normal system of economic arrangements, built on
the natural laws of economic life, to which it would be
the interest and the wisdom of all everywhere to conform.
Further, economic facts are not morally indifferent, as,
for example, astronomical facts are. No moral element
is involved in considering the questions, How many
satellites has Jupiter? or, What is the exact distance
from us of the nearest fixed star? It would be folly to
put these questions as if they involved a moral element,
and say, How many moons *ought* Jupiter to have? or,
How far *ought* the nearest fixed star to be from our
earth?

But if we consider a question in economic science, we
may ask the question simply to find out the fact; as,
How much does a farm labourer receive in Lincolnshire?
or, How much does a seamstress receive in London? But
economic science has a right to consider the moral element,
and to ask, under such conditions of society, How much
ought an agricultural labourer in Lincolnshire to receive?
and, How much *ought* a seamstress in London to receive?

The Socialists of the Chair regard the State, not merely
as an institution for preserving order, and defending its
members from external attack, and from interference with
each other's freedom, but as an institution for doing what-

ever will be beneficial to society, and which can be done better by it than by voluntary individual effort. The State then has a right to promote education, public health, public convenience in transport, and to protect its weaker members, women and children, the aged and the infirm.

Their system is thus opposed to the doctrine of *laisser faire*, to the idea that present evils would in time be removed if every obstruction to the freedom of competition were removed, and that economists have no concern with moral causes. It is also opposed to the various schools that are jealous of State interference, and to the systems of those who, with Herbert Spencer, would make the sole object and duty of the State to administer justice.

The Socialists of the Chair are also opposed to the Democratic Socialists, inasmuch as they condemn revolutionary measures, and believe that society can work out its own salvation without a violent overturning of the present state; they do not seek to establish equality of condition, would permit the possession of private property and the right of bequest, would respect individual liberty, and would not apply the same system always and everywhere. They believe that if their views were carried out, the evils in our present social system would be so mitigated, if not entirely abolished, that Democratic Socialism would of necessity die a natural death.

STATE SOCIALISM.—There is a considerable similarity between the system advocated by the Socialists of the Chair and that known as State Socialism. It has flourished during the last twenty years in Germany. Rodbertus has been its philosopher, Adolph Wagner its exponent, and Prince Bismarck its statesman. It would, however, be a mistake to suppose that this system is an entirely new departure.

In Saint - Simonism we have the elements of State Socialism more clearly expressed than the elements of Christian Socialism. Saint-Simon taught that the State should educate every one, and find employment for all; that education and employment are both universal rights; and that budgets should be so arranged as to provide them for every member of the civil community, so that the "able-bodied man who can get no work" should be an impossibility.

Moreover, from early times the Prussian monarchy had democratic sympathies. Frederick the Great adopted as his motto, "Salus publica suprema lex." He endeavoured to administer even-handed justice, to protect the weak against the strong. He established a governmental department for commerce and manufactures, protected native industries, subsidised native manufactures, and established industrial undertakings, not for the purpose of revenue, but for the enrichment of his country. When asked to sanction a tax on bread and meat, he returned the official document with the note, "I will never agree to make the poor man's bread and meat dear; I am the advocate of the poor."

A similar spirit animated most of his successors. In the early part of the nineteenth century there was for a time the triumph of free trade and individualism; but after a few years there was a return to the former policy. Thus the State Socialism of more recent years has been simply a historical development of the traditional policy of Prussia.

State Socialism differs from individualism, inasmuch as whilst individualism restricts the action of the State to a minimum, State Socialism approves of its action in every matter in which its interference will benefit society.

State Socialism differs from Democratic Socialism, inasmuch as ·Democratic Socialism would subvert the State as it now exists. State Socialism, on the contrary, would accept its present political form, and use it as the instrument more or less efficient for benefiting society. Thus Schmoller says a firm monarchy is a great blessing for a country, when it is bound up with traditions like those of the Prussian monarchy, which recognises its duty.

State Socialism is thus a *via media* between individualism and Democratic Socialism. It has no sympathy with revolution, and puts its faith in reform carried out in accordance with existing institutions, the needs of society, and ethical principles. To use the words of Wagner, "There should be reform which is neither subversion, nor stagnation, nor retrogression." This evolutionary form of Socialism seeks to ameliorate the condition of the working classes, admits the advantages of free competition, but also condemns its serious evils.

Wagner insists on the ethical factor being considered in the settlement of economic problems, and condemns "moral indifferentism in the domain of economic dealings." To his mind the idea of regarding labour power as a commodity, and wages as its price, is not only unchristian, but inhuman in the worst sense of the word."

The claims of the workman as a man should be considered, and provision made for his intellectual and moral culture, for his social activities, for his recreation, and for his enjoyment of a due proportion of the national income. He does not seek, as the Social Democrats do, to abolish social inequalities, but to diminish them.

" What would be taken from the higher classes," Wagner says, " the workman has hitherto had to do- without, with far greater hardship than his more privileged fellow man would in future experience through its loss, for his position would still remain far better than the labourer's."

Prince Bismarck declared, in a speech delivered in January, 1882 : " I do not comprehend with what right we acknowledge the commands of Christianity as binding upon our private dealings, and yet in the more important sphere of our duty—participation in the government of a country having a population of forty-five millions—push them into the background, and say here we need not trouble.   For my part, I confess openly that my belief in the consequence of our revealed religion, in the form of moral law, is sufficient for me. . . . I, the minister of the State, am a Christian, and as such I am determined to act as I believe I am justified before God."

Again he said, in the Reichstag, when answering the questions of the Progressist leader : " Herr Richter has called attention to the responsibility of the State for what it does.   But it is my opinion that the State can also be responsible for what it does not do.   I do not think that doctrines like those of *laisser faire* and *laisser aller,* 'Pure Manchesterdom in politics,' 'He who is not strong enough to .stand must be knocked down and trodden to the ground,'—that doctrines like these should be applied in the State. . . . On the other hand, I believe that those who profess horror at the intervention of the State for the protection of the weak lay themselves open to the suspicion that they are desirous of using their strength—be it that of capital, that of rhetoric, or whatever it be—for the benefit of a section, for the oppression of the rest, for the introduction of party domination, and that they will be chagrined as soon as this design is disturbed by any action of the government."

"Give the labourer," he said, "the right to labour when he is able-bodied; give him the right to relief when he is sick; give him the right to maintenance when he is old: and if you do so, if you do not shrink from the sacrifice, and do not cry out about State Socialism whenever the State does anything for the labourer in the way of Christian charity, then I believe you will destroy the charm of the Wyden (*i.e.* Social Democratic) programme."

State Socialists demand that the rate of wages shall be increased, so that a higher standard of life by workmen may be maintained; that the hours of work shall be diminished, in order to economise the physical strength of the worker, whose life is often shortened, and upon whom premature old age often comes, because of the excessive demands made upon his powers of work and of endurance, also to give him time for intellectual and moral improvement, and for social enjoyment. They also demand, in the interests of morality and religion and health, the abolition of Sunday labour, except in occupations which on technical grounds necessitate continuity of production, or which supply to the public necessary products requiring daily delivery.

Further, they demand that there should be such a supervision exercised over the conditions of labour as would render them free from any injurious influence either on the health or the morals of the worker; that a provision should be made, by State-aided insurance or otherwise, for the maintenance of the worker in times of accident, sickness, or old age.

State Socialists are in favour of co-operation, both in production and in distribution.

They would also lighten the burden on the working classes by a readjustment of taxation. They maintain that taxes ought to be chiefly direct, and only to a slight degree, and mainly on moral grounds, indirect—a tax on alcoholic liquors, for example, to discourage their immoderate consumption; that the necessaries of the poor, if taxed at all, ought to be taxed but slightly; on the other hand, the luxuries of the rich ought to be taxed heavily.   So, too, should the unearned increment, and profits made by Stock Exchange speculation and gambling. They would make legacies and bequests pay a high tribute to the national exchequer.

Regarding the land question, they would give compensation in case of expropriation, but hold that the State ought to have the right of readily expropriating wherever and whenever it can be done to public advantage.   They do not object to private property in land in those cases in which it is not injurious to the public welfare.   They would prefer small estates to be in private hands, but large estates to be held collectively.   Buildings in cities and building ground, forests, as well as all means of communication, such as roads, railways, and canals, should be held collectively.

Insurance against fire, accident, and death ought not to be a means of raising dividends, but, for the sake of security and economical management, ought to be in the hands of the State.

The legislation for the last twenty years in Germany has been of quite a " paternal " character, and entirely in accordance with the principles and objects just stated. It must be admitted that this State Socialism has very lofty and praiseworthy aims, and that it has done much to improve the condition of· the working classes, and to bring many of the comforts and appliances of civilized life within their easy reach. It has not yet, however, solved the social question, nor removed discontent, nor blotted out Democratic Socialism.

CHAPTER V.

WE have spoken of Babœuf as the father of modern
Socialism, and consequently it might have seemed better
to have traced the development of Socialism in France
before tracing it in Germany. On the other hand, the
influence of the great German leaders—Marx and Lassalle
—was so extensive that, in fact, it would be impossible
to follow intelligently the development of Socialism, without some knowledge of their life and opinions; and
therefore we traced the history of Socialism in Germany
first.

We have already reviewed some of the forces operating
in society in France, about the period of the Revolution of
1789. We have now to consider both some other men
and some other ideas, that were important factors in the
development of Socialism in France.

Count Henri de Saint-Simon, who is sometimes spoken
of as the founder of French Socialism, was born in Paris
in 1760. As a volunteer, he assisted the American
colonies in their revolt against Great Britain. He amassed
a little fortune by land speculation, but soon lost it. He
was aided by the generosity of a former valet, accepted a
laborious situation at a salary of forty pounds a year,

attempted to commit suicide in 1823, and died in penury two years after.

His writings were numerous, his system utopian and fantastic. His followers had lax views regarding marriage and the relation of the sexes, "advocated a social hierarchy, in which each man shall be placed according to his capacity, and rewarded according to his works," condemned "the exploitation of man by man," and declared that the aim of society ought to be "the exploitation of the globe by man associated to man." Saint-Simon's views regarding the poor have been already referred to.

About the same time as Saint-Simon, *Fourier* lived. He never had many disciples, yet he can scarcely be left unnoticed, inasmuch as some of his ideas have been developed by subsequent thinkers, more especially in connexion with the form of Socialism known as Communism. In Fourier's *phalange* we have the germ of Communism.

The *phalange* was to consist of four hundred families living on a square league of land. The individuals composing this body were to group themselves according to the dictates of free elective affinity. Each one was to pursue his own course. Love was to be free. Free unions might be formed, which might or might not become permanent. Labour was to be made attractive by frequent change of occupation, and by adaptation to the taste and capacity of the worker. Every one was to be well paid; but necessary work was to be best paid, useful work next, and then pleasant work.

A journal was started to advocate these views, and an attempt was made to establish a *phalange* on lands near.

Versailles; it is almost unnecessary to add that it was a complete failure.

Of a much more practical character was the Socialism of *Louis Blanc.* He was a journalist in Paris, and brought out in his paper, the *Revue du Progrès,* a series of articles, afterwards published as the *Organisation du Travail.* This book, which soon gained great popularity, denounces the evils of competition, and advocates free co-operation and fraternal association. It teaches that social reform could not be obtained without political reform, and hence that the first condition of social amelioration is that the State should be constituted on a thoroughly democratic basis. Louis Blanc was a prominent actor in the Revolution of 1848, when the working classes first obtained political power, and overturned a representative monarchy with a very restricted franchise.

He advocated the establishment of national workshops, for which the State should supply the capital, and the workmen elect directors and managers, and arrange the division of the profits. There was to be little difference in the remuneration given for different kinds of work. "Though the false and anti-social education given to the present generation makes it difficult to find any other motive of emulation and encouragement than a higher salary, the wages will be equal, as the ideas and character of men will be changed by an absolutely new education."

We come now to one whose ideas have done more to mould Socialism, and whose sayings are more frequently quoted, than those of any French Socialist yet named. *Pierre Joseph Proudhon* was born of very poor parents at

Besançon in 1809. He had to borrow his school books from his schoolmates; and it is said that one time he came, laden with prizes, to find that the family resources were exhausted, and that there was no food in his home. He became a corrector for the press, and thereby acquired considerable acquaintance with current literature. In 1838 he obtained from the Academy of Besançon a bursary of fifteen hundred francs a year for three years.

He went to Paris, and there published his first work, *What is Property?* To which question he gives his well-known answer, " La propriété c'est le vol "—" Property is robbery." In the *Représentant du Peuple* he advocated the most extreme theories.

He was elected a member of the Assembly for the Seine Department, and proposed a tax of one-third on all interest and rent, which was carried.

The duration of labour he held to be the just measure of value. The day's labour of one man is the equivalent of the day's labour of any other man; therefore, he concluded, no one man should get more for his day's work than any other man.

" From the great principle of service," says Kirkup, " as the equivalent of service, is derived Proudhon's axiom that property is the right of *aubaine*. The *aubain* was a stranger not naturalized; and the right of *aubaine* was the right in virtue of which the sovereign claimed the goods of such a stranger who had died in his territory. Property is a right of the same nature, with a like power of appropriation in the form of rent, interest, etc. It reaps without labour, consumes without producing, and enjoys without exertion.

Proudhon was anxious that society should rest on the principles of justice and equality. He condemned the immorality of the followers of Saint-Simon and Fourier, and desired the gradual abolition of all property and of all government, so that every man might be in an independent position, and a law unto himself. "Government of man by man, in every form," he says, "is oppression." It is not difficult to see in these sentiments the germ of Anarchism.

Proudhon lived in peace under the Second Empire, until he published a work in which he attacked existing institutions with great virulence. He fled to Brussels, and thus escaped imprisonment. He soon, however, returned to France, and died in 1865.

In France the conditions were favourable to the growth of Socialism. It is stated that few Paris workmen were out of debt. Mr. Malet reported to the English Foreign Office, that as a body they were so dissipated that none of them had grandchildren. Their traditions and instincts were revolutionary. Were it not for the great body of peasant proprietors, who were thrifty and industrious, the history of France would be, even much more than it is, a history of revolutions. The French Socialists adopted practically the Gotha programme; but doing so caused serious divisions in their ranks.

They split up into the Republican Socialist Alliance, the Possibilists, and the Anarchists.

The Anarchists, who are a very active body, consist of a number of small clubs, which agree in little except a desire to have all things in common, and a hatred of all authority, whether vested in king, parliament, or com-

mittee. They engage in a constant guerilla war against
" princes, proprietors, and parsons." One club carries on
the campaign against rent, which in their eyes is theft;
and when a landlord takes legal proceedings against a
member to recover it, his fellow members help him to
remove his furniture and cheat the landlord.

Another club tries experiments in chemistry on the
persons and property of capitalists. Every now and again
we read in the daily papers of an explosion in some
street or building, of an outrage in some church, or
of the assassination or attempted assassination of some
capitalist, which serves to show the continued activity of
the members of this club.

The Socialist Revolutionary Party of France adopted
the following programme at Havre in 1880 :

A. POLITICAL.

1. Abolition of all laws restricting freedom of the press,
of association, or of meeting, and particularly the law
against the International Working Men's Association.
Abolition of " work-books."

2. Abolition of the budget of public worship, and secu-
larization of ecclesiastical property.

3. Abolition of national debt.

4. Universal military service on the part of the people.

5. Communal independence in police and local affairs.

B. ECONOMIC.

1. One day of rest in the week under legal regulation.
Limitation of working day to eight hours for adults.
Prohibition of the labour of children under fourteen, and

limitation of work hours to six for young persons between fourteen and sixteen.

2. Legal fixing of minimum wages every year in accordance with the price of provisions.

3. Equality of wages of male and female labour.

4. Scientific and technical training for all children, as well as their support at the expense of society as represented by the State and the commune.

5. Support of the aged and infirm by society.

6. Prohibition of all interference on the part of employers with the management of the relief and sustentation funds of the working classes, to whom the sole control of these funds should be left.

7. Employers' liability guaranteed by deposit by employers proportioned to number of workmen.

8. Participation of the workmen in drawing up factory regulations. Abolition of employer's claim to punish the labour by fines and stoppages (according to the resolution of the Commune of April 27, 1871).

9. Revision of all agreements by which public property has been alienated (banks, railways, mines, etc.). The management of all State factories to be committed to the workmen employed in them.

10. Abolition of all indirect taxes, and change of all direct ones into a progressive income tax on all incomes above three thousand francs.

11. Abolition of the right of inheritance, except in the line of direct descent, and of the latter in the case of fortunes above twenty thousand francs.

They also agreed that all instruments of production must be transferred to the possession of the community, and that this can only be effected by a revolution on the part of the working classes organized as an independent political party.

Subsequently there has been a split. One party, the Broussists or Possibilists, are practically opportunists, and adopt municipal Socialism as a step towards the establishment of universal collectivism; the other, the Guesdists, aim at the same ultimate object, but would adopt a universal strike and other revolutionary measures in order to obtain it. These two sections are bitter rivals, and rarely work together, either at an election or for any common object.

Then there is an organization called the Revolutionary Union, disciples of Blanqui. In principle they are the same as the Anarchists, but in practice they are more cautious, and rarely put themselves in danger of prosecution or retaliation, so that they have been called "the diplomatists of lawlessness."

In France the Socialists are numerous and active, but they are not so compact a body as they are in Germany.

CHAPTER VI.

In Austria the German-speaking population are to a considerable extent imbued with socialistic ideas. Many of them are of a moderate type, and have never struck " by legal means " out of their programme. At the same time it would appear that a minority of violent Anarchists, led by Penkest, a house painter, who once lived in London, are making more progress than the moderate party. Neither section, however, has a parliamentary representative.

The Austrian peasants are worse off than the same class in other lands, and there is a movement going on amongst them to secure a reduction in their taxation, the abolition of feudal privileges and all rights of birth, gratuitous education, and State help for labour.

They also talk of a peasant State, and say that every minister of the Crown and responsible official should serve an apprenticeship to peasant labour as a qualification for office, in order that he might understand the necessities and capabilities of the peasantry, and sympathise with their troubles, difficulties, and wrongs.

There are similarities and differences, sympathies and antipathies, between those who favour the idea of a peasant

State and those who desire a labour State, so that on the whole the movement amongst the agricultural labourers in Austria is antagonistic to Socialism properly so called.

Many of the nobility and clergy in Austria take an earnest and intelligent interest in the social question, and are doing their best to aid those reforms which would ameliorate the condition of those classes which are suffering from evils that can and ought to be removed by legislation.

In Italy the conditions are peculiarly favourable to the growth of Socialism. In it there is no great industry. The nobles are poor, so are the peasants, so are the working-men. There is a large body of university graduates, well educated, but barely able to make a living.

In striking contrast to the days when Venice was the commercial capital of the world, the employing class lacks enterprise. Instead of helping themselves, the Italians look to the government to help them. The government is the great employer of labour, but has little skill in finance, and is neither successful in its management of monetary affairs, nor its power of maintaining the security of life and property. It is hampered with the heritage of past misgovernment, and with the unsettled relations between it and the Vatican.

"The peasants," says M. de Laveleye, "are reduced to extreme misery by rent and taxation, both alike excessive. Wages are completely inadequate. Agricultural labourers live huddled in *bourgades*, and obtain only intermittent employment. There is thus a rural proletariat more wretched than the industrial. Excluded from property by *latifundia*, it becomes the enemy of a social order that crushes it."

Bakunin, the Anarchist, introduced Socialism into Italy in 1868. It rapidly spread, and was remarkable for the violence of its attacks on the Church, State, and family. In 1878 an attempt was made on the life of the king, which led to the adoption of measures that effectually suppressed, for a time, the socialistic movement. In 1882 a Franchise Act was passed, giving the franchise to one person in every fourteen,—in England one in every six enjoys it,—and the security of the ballot.

Accordingly a Socialistic Labour Party was formed, with which some smaller bodies joined. After a time it was suppressed by the government. It is, however, still active, and in 1890 returned three members to Parliament.

The Anarchists are even more bitterly opposed to this party than the government is, and denounced them as traitors, because they took any part whatever in parliamentary elections. Maletesta, the Anarchist leader, and fifty-three of his companions were imprisoned in 1883 for inciting to disturbance of the public peace.

The Anarchists of Italy are even more prone than other Anarchists to internal disruptions and disputes. M. de Laveleye remarks : " The malaria which makes Rome uninhabitable for part of the year will long preserve her from the danger of becoming the seat of a new Commune."

The International introduced Socialism into Spain in 1868. At first it made rapid progress, and was of a very extreme character. M. de Laveleye visited Spain in the following year, attended several Socialist clubs, and says of them : " They were usually held in churches erected for worship. From the pulpits the orators attacked all that had previously been exalted there—God, religion, the priests, the rich. The speeches were white-hot, but the audience remained calm. Many women were seated on the ground, working, nursing their babies, and listening attentively as to a sermon. It was the very image of '93." He also says that their journals wrote with unparalleled violence against religion and the Church.

The Anarchists calling themselves Autonomists, and led by Bakunin, established their peculiar form of Socialism at Barcelona and other places in Southern Spain. At Carthagena they seized some Spanish ironclads, and for a time held their ground in defiance of the government, but were ultimately put down by the national troops.

In Spain, as elsewhere, there have been many divisions amongst the Socialists. The majority of them, however, are Anarchists.

The Black Hand, with anarchist principles, is a separate association, and committed many outrages in 1881 and 1882. Both the Anarchists and the Black Hand are mainly composed of rural labourers. The artisans of the towns show comparatively little sympathy with the policy or principles of either organization. They have powerful trades unions of their own, and in May, 1890, held a demonstration in opposition to the Socialists, and declared they were in favour of State Socialism, and of State legislation, both domestic and international, to improve the general condition of the working classes, without any revolutionary or sudden change that could alarm the sovereign and the governing classes.

In Portugal, Socialism has had much less success than even in Spain. The climate of Portugal is good, its soil productive, its people fairly comfortable and contented.

M. de Laveleye says that they are "less violent than
the Spaniards; the economic situation of the country is
better, and liberty being very great, prevents the explosion
of popular fury, which is worse when exasperated by
repression."

Socialism has not made any progress worth speaking of
in Norway or Sweden; although, indeed, recent events in
the latter country show that the Socialist propaganda is
at work.

In Denmark there are a large number of peasant proprietors whose holdings are so small as to be insufficient
for their maintenance, so that they are in a condition of
chronic poverty. The working-men, whilst sober and well
educated, according to Mr. Strachey in his report to the
Foreign Office, do not know the meaning of the word
"work." Being deficient in industry and thrift, they are
as a rule badly off. Every fourth person in Copenhagen
was in receipt of parochial relief (1867).

Consequently, the conditions being favourable, Socialism
has made considerable progress. It has one of the best
circulated papers in the kingdom, the *Social Demokraten,*
and has representatives in both houses of Parliament. It
is, however, of a very moderate type, opposed to revolution, and in favour of constitutional agitation.

At its introduction into Belgium and Holland, Socialism
made rapid progress; but, in accordance with what we
have seen occurring so frequently in the history of this
movement, it was split up by internal dissension into
many sections, and is at present in a moribund condition.
In Belgium there is a powerful labour party, which seeks
by practical measures of remedial legislation, and without

violence or revolution, to promote the well-being of the working classes.

Socialism has never made progress in Switzerland. The Socialists who are there are chiefly foreigners. The government, in 1884, expelled several leading Anarchists. They were all either Austrians or Germans, who had abused the hospitality extended to them, not only by planning outrages which shocked all Europe, but also by causing confusion and bloodshed in their adopted home.

Switzerland is a land of liberty; the different classes of society live together in concord; there are many influential and well-managed benevolent societies, so that, whilst it is not a rich country, squalor and want, which are so often found in rich countries, are unknown.

CHAPTER VII.

HISTORY shows us that Russia owes its greatness to its
Tzars. On the part of the mass of the people there is a
touching confidence in the power, wisdom, and love of the
"little Father." This confidence is partly the result of
the traditions of the great things the Tzars have done for
their country, and partly the result of prevailing ignorance
and superstition. In Russia, constitutional government,
constitutional rights and liberties, are unknown ; there is
no freedom of the press, and no right of public meeting.
It is a functionary, not a law, State. "Tyranny tempered
by the fear of assassination," has been given as a fitting
definition of its cruel and corrupt government. Bureau-
cracy of the worst form luxuriantly flourishes, so that
frequently the good intentions of the Tzar have been
delayed or thwarted. It has thus about as bad a government as it is possible for a country to have.

Russia is a land of anomalies and contradictions.
Whilst it suffers from excess of centralization, it yet
possesses that which many revolutionists regard as the
very *summum bonum* of humanity. Every peasant born

in a village and able to work has a right to a fair share of the land. There is a periodical division of it, and the management of local matters is in the hands of the entire village.

Stepniak in his *History of Russia under the Tzars* thus describes a Russian *mir*: "The meetings of the village communes, like those of the *Landesgemeinde* of the primitive Swiss cantons, are held under the vault of heaven, before the starosta's house, before a tavern, or at any other convenient place. The thing that most strikes a person who is present for the first time at one of these meetings, is the utter confusion which seems to characterize its proceedings. Chairman there is none. The debates are scenes of the wildest disorder. After the convener has explained his reasons for calling the meeting, everybody rushes in to express his opinion, and for a while the debate resembles a free fight of pugilists. The right of speaking belongs to him who can command attention. If an orator pleases his audience, interrupters are promptly silenced; but if he says nothing worth hearing, nobody heeds him, and he is shut up. When the question is somewhat of a burning one, and the meeting begins to grow warm, all speak at once, and none listens. On these occasions the assembly breaks up into groups, each of which discusses the subject on its own account. Everybody shouts his arguments at the top of his voice. Charges and objurgations, words of contumely and derision, are heard on every hand, and a wild uproar goes on from which it does not seem possible that any good can result.

"But this apparent confusion is of no moment. It is a necessary means to a certain end. In our village

6

assemblies voting is unknown. Controversies are never
decided by a majority of voices; every question must be
settled unanimously. Hence the general debate, as well
as private discussions, must be continued until a proposal
is brought forward which conciliates all interests, and wins
the suffrage of the entire *mir*. It is, moreover, evident
that to reach this consummation the debates must be
thorough, and the subject well threshed out; and in order
to overcome isolated opposition, it is essential for the
advocates of conflicting views to be brought face to face,
and compelled to fight out their differences in single
combat."

Now, as the population increases, and as the land does
not extend its area, it is evident that each man's share
must become smaller and smaller as the years go on.
Some time ago the average size of a holding was ten
acres, and one-third of this is always fallow. The farms
being thus so small, the farming is of a very inferior kind,
so that, in a large proportion of cases, the land is rather a
drag than a help to the proprietor. In fact, if it were not
that different villages pursue different industries,—thus
there are villages of coopers, villages of tailors, villages
from which the male population go to sea, to the Black
Sea or the Baltic, for a great part of the year,—the
proprietors would not be able to pay their taxes.

They are worse off than the crofters of Scotland, and
have not their remedy. The crofters can emigrate, but the
Russians cannot. Owing to the system of joint responsibility for debt, it is the interest of the members of the
mir to prevent each other from leaving the country. Thus
poverty of a very bitter and constant character prevails.

An enormous proportion of the people have to receive public relief, to keep them from starvation.

The Emancipation Act passed by Alexander II. intensified the distress. The vast number of liberated serfs were simply so many more to be sustained by the land held in common, instead of by the estates of the nobles. This increase in the number of labourers necessarily led to an immediate lowering of wages, so that there was an "all round" levelling down to a condition of extreme poverty.

It is true that the government liberally compensated the gentry when the serfs were liberated, but this did not relieve the situation. The gentry as a whole were heavily in debt to the Crown for mortgages on their land. The redemption money was used for paying these debts, the mortgages were cancelled, the Crown benefited, but little money found its way into the hands of the gentry. Land which scarcely paid when worked by free labour, did not pay at all when labour had to be paid for. Much land went out of cultivation, multitudes of household servants were dismissed, as the gentry, being straitened in their circumstances, were obliged to reduce their establishments, and to economise. Thus the social question reached an acute stage.

It is to be remembered that about one-half of Russia belongs to the Crown, and about one-sixth of it to the nobility. It is thus easy to see that with affluence and extravagance on one side, and grinding want on the other, there must arise discontent and desire for change.

Another cause of discontent in Russia is the condition of the army. The Russian soldiers are badly paid; even when paid at all, their payments are often in arrear.

Whilst badly paid, they are worked hard, and subject to a
very severe discipline, so that disobedience to unreasonable
orders is cruelly punished.   Hence in the army there are
many prepared rather to help the revolution than the
government.

Then there are thirteen millions in Russia who, in the
view of the ruling powers in Church and State, are heretics.
They have opinions somewhat resembling those of the
Society of Friends.   They hold the doctrine of the brotherhood of man, and the duty of mutual help.   Their lives are
innocent, and they are good citizens.   Notwithstanding,
they are, time after time, subjected to violent persecutions.
Their marriages are not recognised, and their civil rights
are denied.

In addition, there are many Poles and Jews, and it seems
sport to the Russians to persecute them.   Thus in Russia
there is always a vast mass of discontent, and ill-treated
and discontented men are the raw material on which
revolutionists work.   It is impossible to tell the number
of the disaffected ; Stepniak says hundreds of thousands or
perhaps even millions.

About half a century ago some young men met together
in the house of a rich merchant in Moscow, to study the
works of Hegel.   They were as devoted in their study of
the works of the German philosopher as another band of
young men were about a century before them in studying
the sacred Scriptures.   From the young men in Oxford
came the great Methodist revival, and from the young men
in Moscow came Russian Socialism.   From Hegel they
were led to Feuerbach, and from his humanism they were
led to Socialism.   Thus the evolution of Socialism followed

exactly the same order of thought in Russia as in Germany. Herzen said Christianity made the slave a son of man; the Revolution has emancipated him into a citizen; Socialism would make him a man.

One of this band of young men was *Michael Bakunin*, the most potent name in Russian Socialism. By birth he was a noble, and in due time became an officer of artillery. He saw so much of Russian tyranny, and of the suffering it caused in Poland, that he left the army and devoted himself to literature. He went to Paris, and there became intimate with Proudhon, and imbibed his anarchic and economic views. He was a man of immense energy, but had not a well-balanced judgment. He despised the middle course, and constantly advocated both extreme views and extreme measures.

There was an attempted revolution under the Emperor Nicholas. It was sternly repressed. As an example, Herzen—another of the band of young men referred to— was banished to the Asiatic frontier, because he remarked in a private letter to his father, read, however, by the government officials, that a policeman had killed a man in the streets of St. Petersburg.

Herzen came to London after the Revolution of 1848, and started a paper called *To Kolokol* (*The Bell*). He was accurately informed of what was going on in Russia, and he criticised with great freedom and ability the action of the government, advocated many needed reforms, and ventilated his philosophical and social opinions.

His views were eagerly adopted by the Russian youth, and Herzenism became a popular system. The Russians, naturally enthusiastic and prone to run to extremes, soon went beyond his teaching. He, living in London and enjoying liberty, became more moderate. The Russians, still oppressed and suffering under the harshness, cruelty, and injustice of the government—for it was impossible for one suspected of disaffection to get a fair trial—evolved the Russian type of Socialism known as' Nihilism.

The word was first employed by Turgenieff in his novel *Fathers and Sons,* where Arcadi Petrovitch surprises his father and uncle by describing his friend Bazaroff as a Nihilist. "A Nihilist!" said Nicholas Petrovitch. "This word must come from the Latin *nihil,* nothing, as far as I can judge, and consequently it signifies a man who recognises nothing."

"Or rather who respects nothing," said Paul Petrovitch.

"A man who looks at everything from a critical point of view," said Arcadi.

"Does not that come to the same thing?" asked his uncle.

"No, not at all. A Nihilist is a man who bows before no authority, who accepts no principle without examination, no matter what credit the principle has."

"Yes; before we had Hegelians; now we have Nihilists. We shall see what you will do to exist in nothingness, in a vacuum, as if under an air-pump."

When, after the death of Nicholas, Alexander II. ascended the throne, the Nihilists expected from him large concessions of popular liberty. They believed that many of the reforms on which their hearts were set would be brought about by the new Tzar; hence they took, not to plotting, but to Sunday schools.

They sought to "make the people," by which phrase

they meant to educate and train the people, so that they might be able to use their liberty wisely when it was granted to them. Filled with zeal in the cause of humanity, they went forth to preach the gospel of humanism. They lived as the poorest lived, dressed shabbily, and wore green spectacles, so that neither in dress, diet, nor appearance might they seem superior to the masses; they laboured hard, taught in Sunday schools, and established reading circles. Tchernycheffsky was the leader in this movement.

When the Emancipation Act was passed, with the results we have already seen, the Nihilists became revolutionary. The pressure of poverty, the disappointment at the conduct of the Tzar, acting upon men who were theoretical Socialists and humanists, naturally led them to form designs, many of them desperate, against the existing order of things, which they found to be intolerable.

In 1862, the government, alarmed at the widespread discontent, adopted repressive measures which greatly aggravated the situation. Sunday schools, reading circles, and liberal newspapers were suppressed. Tchernycheffsky, after an imprisonment of two years without a trial, was sent to the Siberian mines, where he still remains, a living example of the tender mercies of the Russian government. These measures made the party more united and desperate. Bakunin had taken an active part in the disturbances in Dresden in 1849. As the result of doing so, he was for nearly eight years confined in various prisons in Saxony, Austria, and Russia, and was then exiled for life to Siberia. A relative of his was governor there, so that greater liberty was allowed to him than to other prisoners; consequently about this time he escaped and sent emissaries to Russia,

who taught the most extreme doctrines, and urged immediate revolution against the existing social order.

Bakunin came to London; but there was now a wide
divergence between the views of the old friends. The
moderate views of Herzen were not acceptable to Bakunin
or the Russian Nihilists, and henceforth Herzen ceased to
be a power in the Russian social movement. Bakunin
spent his time in promoting conspiracies and advocating
the extremest type of Nihilism, amorphism and pan-
destruction. His brain seems to have been unsettled
by his treatment. With immense energy he pushed on-
ward the revolutionary movement, so that it produced
terror and uncertainty in all the government circles in
Russia, and the Tzar and high officials lived in constant
dread of assassination.

In his *Revolutionary Catechism*—whether written by himself or not, it correctly represents his opinions and those of
his followers—he describes a Nihilist of the extreme type.
"The revolutionist is a man under a vow. He ought to
have no personal interests, no business, no sentiments, no
property. He ought to occupy himself entirely with one
exclusive interest, with one thought, and one passion : the
revolution. . . . He has only one aim, one science:
destruction. For that and nothing but that he studied
mechanics, physics, chemistry, and medicine. He observes
with the same object the men, the characters, the positions,
and all the conditions of the social order. He despises and
hates existing morality. For him everything is moral that
favours the triumph of the revolution, everything is immoral and criminal that hinders it. . . . Between him and
society there is war to the death, incessant, irreconcilable.

He ought to be prepared to die, to bear torture, and to kill with his own hands all who obstruct the revolution. So much the worse for him if he has in this world any ties of parentage, friendship, or love! He is not a true revolutionist if these attachments stay his arm. In the meantime he ought to live in the middle of society, feigning to be what he is not. He ought to penetrate everywhere, among high and low alike: into the merchant's office, into the Church, into the government bureaux, into the army, into the literary world, into the secret police, and even into the imperial palace. . . . He must make a list of those who are condemned to death, and expedite their sentence according to the order of their relative iniquities. . . . A new member can only be received into the association by a unanimous vote, and after giving proofs of his merit, not in words, but in action. Every ' companion ' ought to have under his hand several revolutionists of the second or third degree, not entirely initiated. He ought to consider them part of the revolutionary capital placed at his disposal, and he ought to use them economically, and so as to extract the greatest possible profit out of them. . . . The most precious element of all are women, completely initiated, and accepting our entire programme. Without their help we can do nothing."

Karakozoff made an abortive attempt on the life of the Tzar in the year 1866. This was the death-knell of all hopes of constitutional liberties being granted to the Russians. The very semblance of fair and independent trial ceased. Trials became purely administrative. The powers exercised by local bodies over roads, schools, the poor, and sanitary affairs, were taken away, and everything was controlled by the imperial executive. The private societies of students at the universities were interfered with, their reading and study were confined to what the authorities regarded as safe, and their private lives were carefully watched. Between the years 1873–6 over two thousand arrests were made.

These measures produced their natural fruit. Numerous secret societies, differing mainly on the question what degree of force should be used, sprang into existence. The number and bitterness and determination of the Nihilists increased daily. The works of the German Socialists were eagerly read. Children were baptized in the name of Lassalle.

A young lady, Vera Sassmlitsch, fired at the head of the Russian police in the streets of St. Petersburg. She was tried, and, to the astonishment of all, acquitted. The government attempted to seize her, but she escaped to Switzerland.

Plots, conflicts, and assassinations continually occurred, until the climax came in 1881, when the Tzar himself fell a victim to the vengeance of the Nihilists. Again a young lady appears upon the scene, for it was Sophia Perovskaia who, by the waving of a veil, guided the men who threw the fatal bombs.

The different secret societies, after many unions and divisions, have at length settled down into two principal ones, called "The Will of the People Party," and the "Party of the Black Division."

Both parties are terrorists. The "Will of the People Party" mainly pursues a conflict with the government. The "Party of the Black Division" is the more important.

It has a strong dislike to centralized government, and believes in the Russian *mir.* It is an old idea amongst the Russians, that when by increase of population, or any other cause, it was impossible for the inhabitants to have sufficient land, so that each family might live in some degree of comfort, there should be a division of the whole country, including the enormous estates of the Crown, equal to one-half, and the large estates of the nobles, equal to one-sixth of the empire.

Their objects then are to effect an equitable division of land, to establish local government in communes by an enlargement of the powers already possessed by the *mir,* and to destroy the present system of centralized government. They do not care so much for a constitution as the " Will of the People Party " do ; that, indeed, is the main difference between the two parties.

No sketch of Russian Socialism would be complete without some reference to Prince Kropotkine. He is a member of one of the noblest families in Russia. In his childhood he saw the cruelties practised on his father's serfs, and all his sympathies went out towards the oppressed. He became a page, lived at the imperial court, and learned to hate the aristocracy. He was an eager student, and is a highly cultured man. He joined the Socialists, and was imprisoned in 1882. So barbarous was the treatment of those imprisoned along with him, that nine lost their reason and eleven committed suicide. His health failed, and he was taken to a hospital, from which he escaped to Switzerland. He now lives in London, and is well known as an author.

The economic ideas of Russian Socialism are the same

as those generally received by Socialists. It is, of all forms
of Socialism, the form most in favour of revolution, and
most antagonistic to every kind of government, holding
firmly, in the words of Bakunin, that " it is the peculiarity
of privilege, and of every privileged position, to kill the
intellect and heart of man. The privileged man, whether he
be privileged politically or economically, is a man depraved
in intellect and heart." It objects to all legislation,
authority, and influence, even if it proceeds from universal
suffrage, convinced that every kind of government " must
always turn to the profit of a dominating and exploiting
minority, against the interests of the great majority
enslaved."

CHAPTER VIII.

ROBERT OWEN was born in North Wales in 1771. He was an excellent business man, and had great organizing ability. Although not a believer in Christianity, and having very lax views on the subject of marriage, he was upright and benevolent.

In his time wages were low and employment uncertain. The introduction of improved machinery, the employment of women and children, the long hours of labour, the gross ignorance of the workers, and the absence of protective legislation, caused the lot of the working classes to be one of great hardship. Owen founded infant schools, tried to shorten the hours of labour, took an active interest in factory legislation, and advocated co-operation. He established Socialist settlements, which, however, were not successful.

When Owenism failed, under the guidance of Maurice, Kingsley, Hughes, and others, a Christian Socialist movement was inaugurated, which exercised an ameliorating influence upon society, but did not become a permanent institution in the country.

Although the labourer's condition is vastly better than it was in the days of Owen, and he is now by law protected from many evils from which then he suffered, still there are many things in English society which favour the growth of Socialism.

The landowners are very few. Glaring anomalies exist. For example, the ground landlords of London, the value of whose property has been estimated at over four hundred millions sterling, pay no local rates, and contribute only half a million a year to the imperial exchequer; whilst the tenants who have built the houses, and whose property amounts to about two hundred millions, pay seven millions local rates in addition to income tax and house duty.

Commerce is carried on by great centralized capital. Vast fortunes have been accumulated. Yet the overwhelming majority are proletarians, and every tenth person is in poverty. The differences in the enjoyment of the comforts of life are very marked. The extremes of wealth and squalid poverty are brought close together. For example, eight dock labourers sleep in three beds in one small room, in a stifling atmosphere. The employer of these labourers leases acres of land from a great landowner that he may enjoy a few weeks' shooting.

According to the Rev. Peter Thompson, a woman working hard at sack work for sixteen hours could do a " turn " and a half, earning thereby ninepence. There are twenty sacks in a "turn." By getting one or two children to help her, she could manage to do two turns, and so get one shilling. The woman working at sack work seems to be better off than the woman who works at trouser finishing.

She has to buy her own thread, and oil when it is dark. Working from three o'clock in the morning till ten o'clock at night, she can earn sixpence in the summer; in the winter, light costs about one penny, when her earning is reduced to fivepence.

There are the sweating dens, where the sanitary and moral conditions are infamous, the hours of work long, and the remuneration miserable. In one of these dens a poor girl may work fourteen hours a day and earn six shillings a week, not enough to buy a sufficiency of the coarsest food—not to speak of clothing and other necessary expenditure. The *Song of the Shirt* is not antiquated; it presents a picture of many in every large city to-day. Not very far from these dens are mansions. Those who live in them are surrounded by luxuries from every part of the globe, their every want is anticipated, and their every sense charmed by all that art and wealth can accomplish.

A bishop of the Church of England says: "The zones of enormous wealth and degrading poverty, unless carefully considered, will presently generate a tornado, which, when the storm clears, may leave a good deal of wreckage behind."

Archdeacon Farrar, speaking of the state of London, tells us that "under the very shadow of our abbey there is a vast area of want and vice, of crime and misery, the existence of which it is shameful to ignore, since the facts of it are daily before our eyes, and the proofs of it daily thrust upon our notice. Within a bow-shot even of this place are streets where drink and harlotry are rampant; where men, women, and children live in chronic misery;

where every now and then some terrible crime is perpetrated."

A Salvation Army officer describes the state of things at night between the Temple and Blackfriars. " Here," he says, " I found the poor wretches by the score; almost every seat contained its full complement of six—some men, some women—all reclining in various postures, and nearly all fast asleep. Just as Big Ben strikes two, the moon, flashing across the Thames and lighting up the stone work of the Embankment, brings into relief a miserable spectacle. Here on the stone abutments, which afford a slight protection from the biting wind, are scores of men lying side by side, huddled together for warmth, and, of course, without any other covering than their ordinary clothing, which is scanty enough at the best. Some have laid down a few pieces of waste paper, by way of taking the chill off the stones; but the majority are too tired even for that, and the nightly toilet of most consists of first removing the hat, swathing the head in whatever may be doing duty as a handkerchief, and then replacing the hat."

According to the estimate of General Booth, there are in London fifty-one thousand paupers, thirty-three thousand homeless, and three hundred thousand who are frequently in a state of starvation, and oscillate between eighteen shillings a week and chronic want.

So it appears that in the commercial metropolis of the world, the city in which are merchant princes whose wealth is to be reckoned by millions, there are thousands of the same flesh and blood who are homeless, hungry, cold, and naked, not merely without the luxuries or comforts of life, but destitute of the ordinary conveniences and necessities of decent human existence.

Now when Socialists declare that this inequality is not necessary, that it results from an unjust division of the products of industry, that the wealth of the rich belongs of right to the worker, often engaged in such a bitter struggle with adverse circumstances, we must not greatly wonder if converts are made.

Yet in England Socialism has not made much progress, neither is it of a violent type. Several causes contribute to this state of facts. The large number of persons who are known to take a deep interest in the social problems of the day, and who are honestly anxious to find out and to do what is best for improving the material and moral conditions under which the working classes live; the influence of the Christian Church, which has deep sympathy with the sorrows of the poor, and has many philanthropic agencies giving practical assistance to those in need, seeking out the widow and the orphan, the blind and maimed and sick, and anxious to rescue those who are ready to perish; the amount of liberty enjoyed, so that every class that has a grievance can make it known, and if deserving can enlist popular sympathy, and get it modified or removed; laws that are just, and are indifferently administered. All these things have retarded the growth of Socialism, and have so taken the virulence out of it that fierce revolutionary ideas are in but little favour with the majority of English Socialists.

The first formal appearance of Socialism proper in England was in 1883, when the Democratic Federation changed its name to the Social Democratic Federation, and

7

deliberately adopted the principles of Karl Marx. Its founders were Mr. William Morris, artist, poet, and master printer; Mr. Hyndman, a frequent writer in the press; Mr. Belfort Bax, an eminent author; Dr. Aveling, a popular lecturer, and son-in-law of Karl Marx; and Miss Helen Taylor, step-daughter of John Stuart Mill.

Like Socialists all the world over, the English Socialists cannot agree together. There are three distinct lines of cleavage. Mr. Morris and his followers are revolutionary Socialists. Mr. Hyndman, originally a barrister, but ruined by unlucky operations on the Stock Exchange, has been obliged to take a clerkship in a bank. He is the head and founder of the Social Democratic Federation, accepts the theories of Marx, and is an opportunist. Mr. John Burns, M.P. for Battersea, was formerly Mr. Hyndman's right-hand man; but there has been a breach since the strikes of 1886 and 1887, "so that the names Burns and Hyndman, which at one time seemed inseparable, are now never joined." Mr. Burns apparently desires to pursue a more active policy than Mr. Hyndman approves of.

It is not an easy matter to form an opinion as to the exact number of Socialists in England; that they form a considerable body may be gathered from the fact that on Sunday and Monday, June 22 and 23, 1890, more than ninety Socialist meetings were held in London and fifty in the provinces.

It has several journals, amongst which are weekly papers, *Justice* and the *Commonweal*, and a monthly magazine, *To-Day.*

Whilst the Labour Party has several representatives in

Parliament, there is only one avowed Socialist, Mr. John Burns.

In the Fabian Society there are Socialists of all ranks. It carries on an active propaganda by means of lectures and of publications. In the year ending April, 1889, the number of lectures delivered by its members was upwards of seven hundred. Many of the members are persons of admitted ability; amongst them are Mr. Sidney Webb, Mr. G. Bernard Shaw, Mr. W. Clarke, and Mrs. Besant.

The volume of *Fabian Essays* has been printed both in a library and a popular edition, and has had a very extensive circulation. In the preface to that work their position is clearly laid down by the editor, Mr. Shaw. "The writers are all Social Democrats, with a common conviction of the necessity of vesting the organization of industry and the material of production in a State identified with the whole people by a complete democracy. But that conviction is peculiar to no individual bias; it is a capitol to which all roads lead; and at least seven of them are represented in these *Fabian Essays:* so that the reader need not fear oppression here any more than in the socialized State of the future, by the ascendency of one particular cast of mind."

In addition to the Socialists proper, there are Christian Socialists. Their views are not at all the same as those of the Christian Socialists previously mentioned. Those condemned competition, and wished to establish co-operation both in production and distribution; but they were very jealous of State interference with individual rights, and respected the institution of private property. The modern Christian Socialists have decided leanings towards State Socialism, and would interfere unduly with private property.

We admit the excellence of the motives that influence Canon Shuttleworth, Mr. Headlam, and others, but we do not believe in their wisdom. An honest avowal of Christianity, pure and simple, is more honouring to the gospel of Christ, of which St. Paul declared he was not ashamed, and of which we ought not to be ashamed, and is more likely to attract and to convince honest Socialists, than any assumption of the name of Socialism by what at least looks like a pious fraud. When Christian Socialists talk Christianity, they are told that they are not Socialists; and when they talk Socialism, they are told that they are not Christians: so that they are like the old man and his ass in the fable, attempting to please everybody they please nobody.

Mr. Belfort Bax speaks on this subject with refreshing candour. " If on their intellectual side, as theories of the universe, the older religions are a *non possumus* for us, they are this none the less on their moral side. The local and tribal religions of ancient times were encountered by the newly awakened ethical conscience of the individual as such. Much in them which was natural symbolism to his ancestors was repellent to him. But Christianity itself contains the same opposition in a more developed form. It is useless blinking the fact that the Christian doctrine is more revolting to the higher moral sense of to-day than the Saturnalia or the cult of Proserpine could have been to the conscience of the early Christian. And more than this, the social and humanistic tendencies of the age,

the consciousness of human welfare and human development as ' our being's end and aim,' as the sole object
worthy of human devotion, must instinctively shrink from
its antithesis, the theological spirit; and this despite the
emasculated free Christian and theistic guise in which
the latter may appear at the present time. ' Ye cannot
serve God and humanity ' is the burden of the nobler
instincts of our epoch. But here, again, we see the
intrinsic unity of the several aspects of human life.
What is it which prevents the realization—ay, and even
in most cases the conception—of nobler aims, of a higher
intellectual, artistic, and moral existence for men ? It is
a true saying, that though false ideas may be refuted by
argument, yet only by true ideas can they be expelled.
The true ideal which alone can effectually exorcise the
spectre of the Christian theology from our midst is
unfortunately confined to a few. And why is it so, but
because modern civilization is composed of two classes,
the worshippers of capital and the victims of capital ?
When ' success in life ' is the highest ideal of which the
majority of men are capable, when the condition of a
higher culture is the freedom which the possession of
capital alone can afford, we need indeed scarcely be
surprised that it is so. The higher human ideal stands
in opposition at once to capitalism, the gospel of success,
with its refined art of cheating, through the process of
exchange, or, in short, to worldliness; and to Christianism,
the gospel of success in a hypothetical other life, or, in
short, to other-worldliness. But a glance around at our
various bodies and organizations, charitable or otherwise,
of a Christian character will show that at least two-thirds

of modern Christianity is simply ‘ capitalism ’ masquerading
in a religious guise.   Even where this is not the case,
Christianity is none the less an integral of the *status quo.*
The privileged classes instinctively feel this.   So long as
human aspiration can be kept along the old lines, so
long as the farther gaze of men can be kept directed
heavenward to the cloud-shapes of God, Christ, and immortality, or inward on their own hearts and consciences, and
averted from the earthly horizon of social regeneration,
all will go well.   John Bull’s auxiliary, the minister of
the gospel, or possibly the wife or daughter of John Bull,
must be able to say to him or her who is not blessed
with J. B.’s share of the good things of this life : ‘ What
does it matter, dear brother or sister ?   Why repine ?
’Tis but for a season God has placed us in different
stations in this life ; in the life to come, where we shall
hope to meet by-and-by, all will be well.’   The idea of
the dear brother or sister meeting this consolation in
affliction with the rebuff of Faust—

> Das drüben mag mich wenig kümmern
>
> .   .   .   .
>
> Schlägst du erst diese welt zu trümmern
> Die andre mag danach entstehen,[1]

or something to the same effect, is naturally repugnant
to the *bourgeois* mind.   No, verily ; this bringing down of
religion from heaven to earth belongs not to the present
civilization of expropriation and privilege !

 “ And now a word or two on a point dealt with by
me more fully elsewhere, to wit, on the ethical contra-

[1] I care little about the other side.
If you try first to ruin this world,
The other may afterwards take rise.

diction of our epoch. The moral side of Christianity is
centred in the notions of individual holiness and responsibility to a supernatural being. This ethical side of
Christianity, largely overlaid by other influences during the
Middle Ages, with Protestantism came again prominently
to the fore, has remained so ever since. But now with
the growing sense among all earnest men of social utility
as the end of all human endeavour an ethic based on the
notion of individual likeness to God is in flagrant contradiction, a contradiction which can only be resolved by
its formal surrender.

" Lastly, one word on that singular hybrid, the 'Christian Socialist.' Though the word Socialism has not been
mentioned, it will have been sufficiently evident that the
goal indicated in the present articles is none other than
Socialism. But the association of Christianism with any
form of Socialism is a mystery, rivalling the mysterious
combination of ethical and other contradictions in the
Christian himself. Notwithstanding that the *soi-disant*
Christian Socialist confessedly finds the natural enemies of
his Socialism among Christians of all orthodox denomina-
tions, still he persists in retaining the designation, while
refusing to employ it in its ordinary signification.

" It is difficult to divine the motive for thus preserving
a name which, confessedly, in its ordinary meaning is not
only alien, but hostile to the doctrine of Socialism. Does
the 'Free Christian' want a personal object of reverence?
We can offer him many such, even now. Let him look
eastward at those who have indeed places to lay their
heads, ay, and in some cases mansions and estates, but
who renounce them and court the slow death of imprison-

ment in fortresses and Siberian mines, who flinch not at
the sword, and whose utmost good fortune is the liberty
of preaching their gospel in the dark places of civilization,
and oftentimes amid a poverty unrelieved by even a
Zacchæus. Let them call to mind the massacres of '71,
and the Paris workman who, on being asked for what
he was fighting and dying, replied, ' Pour la solidarité
humaine.'   Or again, let them think of the agèd
Delescluze closing a life of untiring devotion at the
barricades in harness to the last.   Must we for ever insult
the living and lately dead by falling back for our ideal
upon the first century ?   Do nobleness and devotion,
indeed, require to be mellowed by the ' dim religious light '
of ages before we can recognise them as such ?   This,
however, by the way. Our contention is the following.
If by Christianity be meant the body of dogma usually
connoted by the word, it will probably be conceded by
those to whom we refer that it is in hostility to progress.
If, on the other hand, this be not meant, but merely
the ethical principles Christianity is supposed to embody,
then, even if these principles were distinctly and ex-
clusively Christian, which they are not, we challenge them
to show this connexion, or even their compatibility with
Socialism.   If, again, they fail in this, as fail they must,
the whole matter is resolved into one of sentiment.   And
for the sake of retaining a catchword, for such it is, and
no more, under these circumstances, they would compromise principles, and throw a sop to respectability in
its most hypocritical form.   To say nothing of the
thousands in Europe to whom the name Christian is
positively abhorrent, how shall they face the Eastern

world when the time comes for so doing? Only those
who can tell the Moslem, the Buddhist, the Confucian,
'We care not for Jesus of Nazareth any more than for
Mohammed, for Gautama, or for Kon-fu-tze; disputes as
to the relative merits or demerits of those teachers are
vain as they are endless': only those who can say, 'We
know of greater men than these—greater, inasmuch as
they have not posed as great teachers, but have contented
themselves with the rank of humble and equal workers—
who came in the form of neither God nor prophet, but
of the humanity whose religion is human welfare, not
the welfare of a race or a class, but of the whole; whose
doctrine is its attainment, through human solidarity, or, in
other words—Socialism': only those, we repeat, will ever
obtain the ear of the Orient, and never they who come
in the hated and bloodstained name of Christianity—
name indicative of racial and religious rivalry. What in
earlier phases of human evolution has been accomplished
as in prehuman evolution by the survival of the fittest
in the struggle for existence—in other words, what has
been hitherto accomplished physically or unconsciously,
must, in the future, be done physically or consciously:
the struggle for existence must give place to co-operation
for existence; and this co-operation, though in one sense
the result of economical revolution, implies, on another
side, a correlative change in the basis of ethics and religion.
Then, and not till then, will the contradiction of our age
be resolved in the unity of a fuller and more complete
life than any yet experienced by humanity."

Fidelity to truth should make us ever speak of Christianity and Socialism as distinct and, in many grave respects,

antagonistic systems. Compromise is impossible. When Socialism loses its objectionable elements, it ceases to be Socialism, as it is presented to us by its acknowledged advocates and exponents.

There are also two other societies that aim at the nationalization of the land: one is "The Land Nationalization Society," founded by the well known naturalist Mr. A. R. Wallace, which would take the land from the present owners and give them compensation; the other is "The English Land Restoration League," which would confiscate the rights of the present owners by a system of taxation.

In Ireland there is practically speaking no organized Socialism. The views of Mr. Henry George have been widely spread by Mr. Michael Davitt, the father of the Land League; there are also large numbers who have not clear ideas as to the distinction between *meum* and *tuum*, are not certain that taxes and ordinary debts ought to be paid, but are certain that rent ought not to be paid.

There is also on the part of the artisan population a growing desire for shorter hours of labour, better homes, more material comforts, greater facilities for technical education, and higher wages; but nobody of any importance has adopted distinctly Socialist principles or joined with any of the great Socialist organizations.

A great many experiments in establishing Socialist settlements have been tried in the United States of America, but no one of them has been so successful as to demand our attention. They do not aid us in considering the development of Socialism, although they may hereafter have some value in helping to show its practical impossibility.

Amongst the Germans in the United States a Socialistic Labour Party was founded in 1877 under the auspices of the International, which had transferred its general council to New York in 1872. John Most, having joined them on his expulsion from Germany, caused a division, and headed the secession of the Anarchists. They had a congress in 1883, when they had thirty-eight branches and two thousand members. They held a congress in Pittsburg, and formed themselves into "The International Working People's Association." The following is their programme :

"What we would achieve is therefore plainly and simply—

"1. Destruction of the existing class rule by all means ; *i.e.* by energetic, relentless, revolutionary, and international action.

"2. Establishment of a free society based upon co-operative organization of production.

"3. Free exchange of equivalent products by and between the productive organizations without commerce and profitmongery.

"4. Organization of education on a secular, scientific, and equal basis for both sexes.

"5. Equal rights for all, without distinction of sex or race.

"6. Regulation of all public affairs by free contracts between the autonomous (independent) communes and associations resting on a federalistic basis."

There are not twenty socialist, whereas there are five

hundred labour, newspapers in the United States. The trades unions ignore Socialism. The "Noble Order of the Knights of Labour" expressly repudiates it.

The labour problem in America turns on the question of how to apportion profits, so that labour may get a larger proportion, at the expense of the wages of superintendence, and of the interest for capital invested. Better wages, rather than expropriation of capitalists, either in land or in commerce, occupies the working class mind. Breathing the air of liberty, they believe that they can, without a revolution, work out a condition of things, in which there will be an equitable distribution to every man.

A number of admirers of Mr. Bellamy's fanciful and vapid novel, *Looking Backward,*—the utopian and absurd dream of the practical nineteenth century,—have formed a society, and issued an organ called *The New Nation.* The movement it advocates is "nationalism." Its practical programme is a very modest one. The movement, however, is not likely to extend, or even to exist for any length of time.

A much abler book, written by a much abler man, has had a far greater effect. *Progress and Poverty,* written by Mr. Henry George, has had an immense circulation, and has gained many zealous apostles for the views it contains. The squalid misery of great cities appalled and tormented him, so that he could not rest, thinking of what caused it, and of how it might be cured. He says: "Where the conditions to which material progress everywhere tends are most fully realized,—that is to say, where population is densest, wealth greatest, and the machinery of production and exchange most highly developed,—we find the deepest poverty, the sharpest struggle for existence, and the most enforced idleness."

He saw, or at least he thought he saw, that under the present constitution of society it was necessary that things should grow worse rather than better ; that the rich should become richer, whilst the poor became poorer.

" In the United States," he says, " it is clear that squalor and misery, and the vices and crimes that spring from them everywhere, increase as the village grows to the city, and the march of development brings the advantages of improved methods of production and exchange. It is in the older and richer section of the Union that pauperism and distress are becoming most painfully apparent. If there is less deep poverty in San Francisco than in New York, is it not because San Francisco is yet behind New York in all that both cities are striving for ? When San Francisco reaches the point where New York now is, who can doubt that there will also be ragged and barefooted children in her streets ? "

This view of matters had more than a momentary effect upon Mr. George's mind, for it led him to renounce his religious belief. " It is difficult," he says, "to reconcile the idea of human immortality with the idea that nature wastes men by constantly bringing them into being where there is no room for them. It is impossible to reconcile the idea of an intelligent and beneficent Creator with the belief that the wretchedness and degradation which are the lot of such a large proportion of human kind result from His enactments ; while the idea that man, mentally and physically, is the result of slow modifications perpetuated by heredity irresistibly suggests the idea that

it is the race of life, not the individual life, which is the
object of human existence.   Thus has vanished with many
of us, and is still vanishing with more of us, that belief
which in the battles and ills of life affords the strongest
support and the deepest consolation."   He however, by
his enquiry into the relation between poverty and progress, found more than increased knowledge of his subject,
or his fancied remedy.   "Out of this enquiry," he says,
"has come to me something I did not think to find, and
a faith that was dead revives."

Mr. George states that the object of his enquiry is "the
law which associates poverty with progress, and increases
want with advancing wealth."

Nationalization of the land is the proposed remedy.
The abolition of rent is the panacea for all our ills.   The
" United Labour Party " was founded in 1886 to promote
these views.   In 1887 it expelled Socialists from its ranks.
Mr. George does not regard himself as a Socialist : yet his
system is semi-Socialism.   It is Socialism applied to land.
Some of the many fallacies involved in this scheme we
shall examine at length, when we come to consider the
economic ideas of Socialism.

We have now reviewed the origin of Socialism, its
eventful history, its thinkers, workers, and apostles, its
developments and modifications as it came in contact
with different peoples, religions, governments, and economic
conditions, and consequently we are in a position to consider its economic ideas, its principles, its methods, and its
motives, especially as they are related to Christianity.

CHAPTER IX.

The supposed Sanction that Christianity gives to Socialism—Common Fund of Christ and the Apostles—Communism in Jerusalem—The young Ruler—Can make all Poor, but not all Rich—Dives and Lazarus—Divide the Inheritance—The Family at Bethany—Slavery—Onesimus and Philemon—Christianity sanctions Private Property.

ALREADY we have referred to Christian Socialists in Germany and in England, and we have found that their claim to be regarded as Socialists has been repudiated, in most vigorous language, by Democratic Socialists. They have also been condemned as bad interpreters of Holy Scripture.

We shall now deal with their assertion that Christianity sanctions some of the leading economic ideas of Socialism. It is necessary to do so. There are many, besides those who regard themselves as Christian Socialists, who have a vague impression that Christianity teaches equality of condition, is opposed to the holding of private property, and in favour of a community of goods. In support of these views the fact is adduced that our Lord and the apostles had a common fund; and that as Christians ought to follow their example, therefore Christians, at any rate, ought to have "all things common."

Whilst it is true that there was a common fund out of which were defrayed certain expenses connected with the college of apostles, and of which fund one of their number,

111

Judas Iscariot, was the dishonest treasurer, for he bare the bag, and took for himself what was put therein, still we have no evidence to show that this having a common fund was designed to be an example to us.

Their having this common fund did not prevent the apostles from holding private property. It is clear that St. John had means of his own, and that St. Peter held private property, at least in his boat and appliances for fishing.

Now-a-days men often associate themselves together, and have a common fund to defray the expenses connected with a special work; but each one has besides his own private property. As members of the great Foreign Missionary Society we have a common fund, and expenses connected with the work are paid out of the mission fund: but that does not mean that all members of the Missionary Committee are sustained by the fund, and that they have no income of their own separate and distinct from the income of the Missionary Society; nor even does it mean that the missionaries sent out and sustained by the society may not have private revenues of their own, with which the society has nothing whatever to do. Consequently the fact that our Lord and the apostles had a common fund neither condemns individualism nor sanctions collectivism.

The action of the early disciples in Jerusalem is brought forward. They sold their possessions. They laid the proceeds at the apostles' feet. No man said that any of the things he possessed was his own. They had all things common. Here, it is said, we have a distinct instance of Christian communism. Here is the example the Christian Church should have followed. If it had done so, private property and its resultant evils would have been unknown, at least in Christendom.

Now the action of these early disciples was simply a temporary expedient to meet exceptional circumstances, and as such was certainly allowable. If a number of Christians in any place, in a time of distress or persecution or famine, choose voluntarily to follow their example and have all things common, so as to help one another, they have a right to do so.

It is, however, to be observed that no divine command was given to establish this community of goods. No slightest hint was given that it was designed to be an example to all Christians everywhere. Even whilst the disciples were engaged in carrying out their plan, St. Peter in express terms asserts the lawfulness of holding private property. He said to Ananias, " Whiles it remained, did it not remain thine own ? and after it was sold, was it not in thy power ? "—evidently implying that he need not have sold his property, if he had not wished to sell it; and that after he had sold it, he could do what he liked with the proceeds. No pressure was used, no force of moral obligation was employed, in order to lead Ananias to dispose of his property. It was a spontaneous act. So with the others. They impulsively, under the influence of kindly feelings, but with very questionable wisdom, established this community of goods.

This earliest experiment in Christian communism, like all subsequently made, was an economic failure. Not a chronic plethora of goods, which they had doubtless fondly hoped, but a chronic poverty was the consequence. The practical result is seen in the fact, that after this rash

8

experiment a collection has to be made throughout the
Gentile world, to help the poor saints in Jerusalem.

The incident of the young ruler is supposed to teach the
same false political economy. He came to Jesus, and wanted
to be told what good thing he might do, so that he might
inherit eternal life. In all likelihood he belonged to the
"what can I do more?" sect of the Pharisees. Jesus told
him to sell all that he had—and he had great possessions
—and give to the poor, and follow Him; and that then
he should be a disciple.

Now Jesus did not tell all who came to Him to sell their
possessions, and give all they had to the poor. He did not
tell Nicodemus, another rich Pharisee, to do this, nor did
He tell Zacchæus, the rich publican. Why then did He tell
the young ruler to do it? Christ had a moral purpose in
view. He saw that the great sin of that young ruler was a
common sin,—probably the commonest sin of the Pharisees,
a common sin of the Jewish people, perhaps more markedly
a sin of the Jews than of any other people, not excepting
the Anglo-Saxons, British and American,—the sin of
avarice. The same purpose that led Jesus to ask the
woman of Samaria where was her husband, led Him to
tell the young ruler to sell his possessions; and that
purpose was to produce a self-revelation of character, a
conviction of sin.

Thus the command to sell all that he had and give to
the poor does not express a universal duty, but is a specific
command, given with a specific moral purpose. To draw a
universal obligation from a specific command is a mistake
in morals similar to the common error in logic of drawing
a universal conclusion from a particular premiss. It would

be as reasonable to argue, Aristides was just, therefore all men are just, as to argue that because this rich young ruler was told to sell all that he had and give to the poor, therefore every man who wishes to be one of Christ's disciples should do the same.

The teachings of our Lord are never in opposition to those of common sense. If all rich men were to sell their possessions and give to the poor, the number of the poor would rapidly increase. All the indolent would join their ranks, and would not work until all available supplies were consumed. Then there would be plenty of poor and *no rich.* It is absurd to interpret our Lord's words as teaching us to practise indiscriminate charity, which very brief reflection and a very slight knowledge of human nature show us must lead to the destruction of industry and thrift, and bring all into a condition of hopeless poverty.

The story of Dives and Lazarus is also instanced as showing, that in the view of the great Teacher it is wrong to be rich. No sin is charged against Dives, but the single one that he was rich. Abraham is represented as saying to him: "Son, remember that thou in thy lifetime receivedst thy good things, and Lazarus evil things: but now he is comforted, and thou art tormented."

Now, if the true interpretation of this be that Dives was lost because he was rich,—had received his good things in his lifetime,—then it follows that Lazarus was saved because he was poor,—had received evil things in his lifetime. Then it follows that the richer a man is, the less chance he has of salvation; and the poorer he is, the more certain of it. It is therefore a much better thing to be poor than to be rich, for no amount of temporal wealth can be so valuable as salvation. Consequently no true friend of the poor would try to improve their condition, for in so doing he would be imperilling their salvation. This would be a settlement of the labour question that Socialists at any rate would not desire.

Again, is it not rather strange that Abraham should teach that wealth is a reason for exclusion from heaven, and poverty a reason for admission to it? If wealth keeps out of heaven, how did Abraham get in? The Father of the Faithful and the Friend of God was rich in flocks and herds, and had a full share of temporal prosperity.

Abraham says in answer to Dives, whose success in this instance does not encourage us to believe in the value of the invocation of the saints, "They have Moses and the prophets, let them hear them." Now Moses and the prophets certainly taught that temporal prosperity was a thing to be desired, that it was laudable to pray for it and to work for it, and that its possession was to be regarded as an evidence of the Divine favour. Did they not chant in the temple service?—

Blessed is the man that walketh not in the counsel of the wicked,
Nor standeth in the way of sinners,
Nor sitteth in the seat of the scornful.
But his delight is in the law of the Lord;
And in His law doth he meditate day and night.
And he shall be like a tree planted by the streams of water,
That bringeth forth its fruit in its season,
Whose leaf also doth not wither;
And whatsoever he doeth shall prosper.

It is evident, then, that whatever this story may teach, it does not teach that Dives was lost because he was rich, or because he was dressed in purple and fine linen, and

fared sumptuously every day; or that Lazarus was saved
because he was sick, poor, and friendless.

What, then, was the sin of Dives? It was that, whilst
he was clad in purple and fine linen, and Lazarus was in
rags and covered with sores,—that whilst he fared sumptuously every day, and Lazarus desired to be fed with the
crumbs that fell from his table,—that whilst he was inside
enjoying himself, and Lazarus at his gate in bitter distress,
—he yet made no enquiry about his poor neighbour, and
made no effort to relieve his destitution. Selfish indifference to the sufferings of humanity was the damning sin
of Dives, as it is that of thousands in Christendom to-day,
who, engrossed in their own personal gratification, do not
"consider the poor," and are deaf to the wail of woe that
rises from the cabins, and tenement houses, and slums,
and homeless wanderers, and casual wards of earth, and
reaches, as of old, the ears of the Lord God of Sabaoth.

There was one occasion in our Lord's life when He had
a fitting opportunity for condemning the holding of private
property if He desired to do so. "One out of the multitude
said unto him, Master, bid my brother divide the inheritance
with me. But He said unto him, Man, who made Me a
judge or a divider over you? And He said unto them,
Take heed, and keep yourselves from all covetousness."
Our Lord does not say that neither the one brother nor
the other ought to have had the inheritance; He declines
to interfere in the matter, and refers them to the proper
courts for deciding such matters; for His saying, "Who
made Me a judge?" implies that there is a judge, and
that they should go to him for his decision. Then He
goes to the root of the matter, and exhorts them to beware

of covetousness. Covetousness in His view led to this dispute. He does not say on whose side it was. It may have been ou both sides. Each brother probably wanted more than he was equitably entitled to. If each one had simply wanted a fair proportion, there would have been no dispute, and no need to go to any "judge or divider."

Covetousness on the part of capitalist or of labourer, or of both, covetousness on the part of landlord or of tenant, or of both, is the source of all disputes regarding the division of the proceeds of industry or of agriculture.

Our Lord's reply to this man is a tacit yet distinct sanction of the rightfulness of holding private property. The same approval is implied in the command, "Thou shalt not steal," and in St. Paul's words in the Epistle to the Ephesians, "Let him that stole steal no more." Here God puts the sanction of His law around each man's possessions.

Socialists ask, Who are the thieves? They try to show that the capitalists have taken from the labourer what ought to have been his, and that therefore "property is robbery." Whilst it is true that capitalists have often acquired wealth by unjust means, and have violated this command, in doing so they are condemned by Christianity as emphatically as other thieves, for Christianity, like its Author, is no respecter of persons; yet that St. Paul does not refer to capitalists, but to vulgar thieves, is evident, for he says, "Let him that stole steal no more: but rather let him labour, working with his hands the thing that is good, that he may have whereof to give to him that hath need."

Not only is the moral excellence of many possessors

of private property, under the Mosaic dispensation, admitted and extolled, but under the Christian dispensation many of the early disciples held private property, and it is not intimated that they were in any degree faulty in so doing.

Martha and Mary and Lazarus, whom Jesus loved, were evidently in easy circumstances; they, or one of them, owned the house in which Jesus lodged, where Mary anointed Him with the perfume " genuine and exceeding costly," worth about ten pounds sterling; the tomb hewn in a rock, in which Lazarus was buried, could only be procured by a family having considerable resources.

There were saints in Cæsar's household. Joanna, the wife of Chusa, Herod's steward, was a believer. Lydia was a devout and devoted woman, yet carried on a lucrative business. Theophilus was a man of exalted rank. Amongst the Corinthian believers there were several who exhibited their wealth in an objectionable and ostentatious manner. Judging from the extent of their hospitality, the household of Chloe, " Gaius mine host and of the whole Church," and Philemon with whom St. Paul lodged, must have been well off. From these cases, as well as from others, we conclude that a man may be a sincere follower of Christ and yet hold private property. The right of holding private property is thus sanctioned by Christianity.

It may be said in answer : By the same reasoning slavery could be justified, because many good men held slaves—Philemon, for example. Now if his holding private property shows that Christianity sanctions the holding of private property, then his holding slaves shows that Christianity sanctions slavery.

This answer deserves examination. There is an important difference in the way in which the New Testament speaks of private property and of slavery. It expressly admits the moral right of holding private property; it never admits expressly the moral right of holding slaves. When St. Peter said to Ananias, " Whiles it remained, did it not remain thine own ? and after it was sold, was it not in thy power ? " he expressly admitted the moral right of holding private property.

The case of slavery is different. The moral right of holding slaves is not asserted. Take the fullest statement on this subject that we have in the New Testament, St. Paul's Epistle to Philemon. When St. Paul sent Onesimus, who had robbed and run away from his master, Philemon, back to him, with a beautiful and touching letter, he does not say a word implying that the slave had done wrong in running away from slavery. He implies that, if he had chosen, he might, so far as moral obligation was concerned, have kept Onesimus with him at Rome, " whom I would fain have kept with me: . . . but without thy mind I would do nothing."

Moreover St. Paul tells Philemon to receive him "not as a servant, but as a brother beloved." In this is contained a principle which necessarily must be, and which historically has been, fatal to slavery. From the moment it was declared that masters and slaves were brethren in Christ, slavery was doomed.

Further, St. Paul delicately but distinctly hints that Philemon should formally and legally manumit Onesimus. " Having confidence in thine obedience I write unto thee, knowing that thou wilt do even beyond what I say."

Thus whilst we admit that our Lord and the apostles did not definitely attack slavery, they do not express approval of it, and they lay down principles which are absolutely incompatible with it. Hence wherever Christ reigns slavery has been abolished.

It is otherwise with private property: the moral right to hold it is admitted, and no principle or precept of Christianity is violated by its possession.

CHAPTER X.

SOCIALISTS condemn Christianity because they say it is an
enemy to the progress of humanity, inasmuch as it teaches
men to be content with such things as they have; whereas
progress results from discontent with things as they are,
and the consequent determination to alter and improve
them. Christianity teaches men to be patient under sufferings, remembering that there will be compensations in a
future life, that the things that are seen are temporal, but
that the things not seen are eternal.

There is no doubt that Christianity has led multitudes
to be patient and contented, knowing that in heaven they
have a better and an enduring substance; and in so doing
it has added incalculably to the sum-total of human
happiness.

Neither can there be any doubt that in many cases the
decay of religious belief has led to Socialism; for when
men have lost faith in any real personal immortality, the
natural result is that, believing they have only one life,
they are determined to make the best of it—making the
best of it meaning that they, by right means or wrong, put

themselves into a position that enables them to give the most satisfactory answers to the questions, "What shall I eat? what shall I drink? wherewithal shall I be clothed?"

"If in this life only we have hope," then we naturally should be disposed to accept the statement that "the wisest man is he who so lives as to secure the greatest number of agreeable sensations." Socialism, by emphasising the importance of this present life, is the friend of human progress; Christianity, by emphasising the importance of the life to come, is its enemy.

Let us consider this charge—Is Christianity the enemy of human progress?

It must be admitted that there have been periods in the history of the Church, and there probably always have been sections of the Church, in which views unfriendly to the progress of society have prevailed. Mistaken ideas of spirituality have obtained, and it has been supposed to be unworthy for a Christian even to desire to improve the ordinary conditions of existence. Comfort was denounced as sinful self-indulgence and luxury; cleanliness even has been regarded as a base pandering to fleshly desires; and a wish to rise in the world and possess independent means as covetousness, which is idolatry. Agriculture was regarded as a legitimate method of gaining a living, and it was said of it, "Deo non displicet"; but trade was disparaged, and of the merchant it was said, "Deo placere non potest." Poverty was regarded as closely connected with holiness, and perpetual discomfort was an eminent auxiliary to a religious life. These ascetic ideas largely prevailed during the Middle Ages; in a less or more modified form they largely prevail still. Now it is evident that in proportion as these ideas permeate Christianity, in that degree Christianity will be inimical to the progress of society.

We must enquire, Are these ideas part and parcel of the teaching of Christ and the apostles?

In order to prove that the negative answer to this question is the correct one, we shall establish the proposition that Christianity teaches us, that it is right for us to desire temporal prosperity. Not that it is right for us to desire temporal prosperity above everything else: it ought not to·stand first either in order of time, or in order of importance. " Seek ye *first* the kingdom of God, and His righteousness," is our Lord's command. But in its place and in its degree, and in submission to the will of God, temporal prosperity is a legitimate object of desire. Christ teaches us that a reasonable self-love is right, and that selfishness, which is wrong, is excessive self-love. Vices we may regard as unbalanced and excessive virtues. Self-respect is a virtue; but its excess, pride, is a vice. Thrift is a virtue; but its excess, niggardliness, is a vice. Self-love is right; but its excess, selfishness, is not only wrong, but the parent of many wrongs. Rational self-love is a phrase favoured by many moral philosophers, and implies that the sentient being who does not desire his own happiness is not a reasonable being. If reason reigns, self-love exists; if self-love does not exist, reason has been dethroned. Hence it follows that rational self-love is the accompaniment and evidence of the rule of reason.

This is implied in the divine command that we are to love our neighbour *as* ourselves. Now if we are not to love ourselves at all, it follows that we are not to love our neighbour at all. We are thus taught that rational self-love is a legitimate principle of life and action.

Dr. Harris beautifully says: " There is, be it observed, a wide difference between selfishness and legitimate self-love. This is a principle necessary to all sentient existence. In man it is the principle which impels him to preserve his own life and promote his own happiness. Not only is it consistent with piety, it is the stock on which all piety, in lapsed man, is grafted. Piety is only the principle of self-love carried out in the right direction, and seeking its supreme happiness in God. It is the act or habit of a man who so loves himself that he gives himself to God. Selfishness is fallen self-love. It is self-love in excess, blind to the existence and excellence of God, and seeking its happiness in inferior objects by aiming to subdue them to its own purposes."

As then it is right for us to desire our personal happiness, it must be right for us to desire those things that promote it.

Physical health promotes our personal happiness as well as our independence and our usefulness to others ; therefore it is right for us to desire physical health. But if it be right for us to desire health, it must be right for us to desire those things without which it is, as a rule, practically impossible. In order to have health we require means that will enable us to secure such a dwelling, such clothing and diet, as are essential to its continuance. It is therefore evident that it is right for us to desire temporal prosperity, which implies all those things.

God has given us certain tastes and appetites. That He has provided objects that can gratify them is not only an evidence of design in creation, but of our Creator's great goodness ; " His tender mercies are over all His works."

So long as we obey the moral laws of our being, it cannot be wrong for us to gratify those tastes and appetites. To suppose that it would be wrong to do so would imply, if not that God was the author of evil, at least that He was the great tempter to evil. He has given us an eye that can be charmed with the beautiful in form and colour, and He has given us in rich abundance the beauty that can charm the eye. He has given us tastes that can be gratified with fruits and flowers, and the fruits and flowers that can gratify those tastes. He has given us faculties that can be charmed with the harmony of sweet sounds, and faculties that enable us to produce those sounds.

It must then be right to desire the gratification which God in the great scheme of creation has provided for us ; we must not make Him the minister of sin. Therefore it must be right for us to desire that temporal prosperity which will enable us to procure those enjoyments.

In perfect accord with these views are the example of Christ and the testimony of Scripture. Our Lord was not an ascetic. He contrasted Himself with John the Baptist. " For John the Baptist is come eating no bread nor drinking wine. . . . The Son of man is come eating and drinking." Christ was at the marriage feast in Cana of Galilee, at the " great feast " in Levi's house, and defended the woman who had the " cruse of exceeding precious ointment, and poured it on His head," from those economists who said it might have been sold for three hundred pence—about ten pounds—and given to the poor. St. Paul tells us, " Godliness is profitable for all things, having promise of

the life which now is, and of that which is to come." "Say
ye of the righteous, that it shall be well with him: for
they shall eat the fruit of their doings," says the evangelical prophet. "My son, eat thou honey, for it is good; and
the honeycomb, which is sweet to thy taste," is the counsel
of the book of Proverbs. In Ecclesiastes we read, "Go thy
way, eat thy bread with joy, and drink thy wine with a
merry heart; for God hath already accepted thy works."

Analogy teaches us the same truth. The favourite
figure under which the great Teacher presents God to us
is that of Father. "If ye then, being evil, know how to
give good gifts unto your children, how much more shall
your Father which is in heaven give good things to them
that ask Him?" Here God is shown to us as wiser and
kinder than the wisest and kindest earthly father.

Now what father would not like to see his children
happy, and enjoying his gifts and the pleasures he had
provided for them? Rejection of his gifts, determined
gloom, would not be what the father's heart would desire.
Neither does our great heavenly Father wish us to turn
away from these gifts of His providence which He has
given us richly to enjoy. We please Him most when we
carry out His wishes, not when we despise His gifts in a
voluntary humility and will-worship and dishonouring of
the body.

It is then right for us to desire—in all submission
to God's will—temporal prosperity; and if so, it follows
that it is right to work for it and to enjoy it. This part
therefore of the Socialists' objection to Christianity is not
sustained.

Socialists, as the friends of humanity, point to the evils

in our present social system. They show that to multitudes life is a toil and burden bereft of thought and noble endeavour; that masses of men have to work hard for very little remuneration; that they have to live in crowded, dark, dismal, and unhealthy habitations, where the decencies of life cannot be observed, where neither art nor music can exercise their elevating influence, where the sanitary arrangements are such as to make health impossible and " pestilence to stalk through the land "; that they have neither leisure for mental improvement nor social enjoyment nor needful recreation, so that body and mind alike lose their elasticity; that they cannot obtain sufficient nourishment to enable them to get through their daily toil, and to live as long as they might, considering their original constitution; that many willing to work cannot get anything to do. Carlyle, pointing to one of this class,—the great army of the unemployed,—says, " A man willing to work and unable to find work is, perhaps, the saddest sight that fortune's inequality exhibits under the sun." Socialists point to all these things and say, Christianity is not the friend of humanity; for it makes no effort to remedy those evils.

Again we contend that the charge is true only in so far as Christianity has been misrepresented by Christians; for the example and teaching of Christ show that Christianity, as it ought to be, is entirely free from all blame. We must distinguish between two meanings of the word Christianity. We have Christianity as it was presented and taught by Christ and the apostles, and Christianity as it is presented in the lives and professions of His followers in different lands and ages. In this latter sense Christianity has been often to blame for taking but little interest and making but slight efforts to secure the progress of society.

Let us take the example and teaching of Christ as showing us what ought to be the attitude of Christianity in the presence of the many and crying evils of society. Christ was not heedless of the sick, He healed the stone-mason with the useless hand, He healed Peter's wife's mother of her fever, He healed the impotent man at the pool of Bethesda, He cleansed lepers, He opened the eyes of the blind and unstopped the ears of the deaf. " He healed them that had need of healing." He showed us that the truest charity is to help a man to help himself. His wonderful life, heralded by the angels' song, " Peace on earth and goodwill amongst men," and wound up with what seems like an echo of that song, " Father, forgive them ; for they know not what they do," might have the intervening years between the cradle and the cross summed up in the phrase, " He went about doing good." Whoever else has been indifferent to the sorrows of humanity, Christ was not. Now look at His teaching. If we contrast the teaching of the modern evangelical school with that of Christ, we must say that His teaching was much more practical, and dealt with the duty of brotherly love and mutual help to a larger extent than the evangelical or any other pulpit at present does.

The second great commandment He says is, " Thou shalt love thy neighbour as thyself." Love, yes ; yet not merely the sentiment of love, not merely kindly words, but kindly deeds. He shows us what He means in the parable of the good Samaritan. The priest and the Levite pass by on the other side ; but he who loves his neighbour goes to him in

9

his distress, and does not merely weep over him or wax eloquent over his woes, but helps him—helps him largely, helps him efficiently : that was Christ's idea of what a Christian ought to do.

Then look at Christ's representation of the final judgment. How much depends on what the man has done for his fellow-men ! How marvellously Christ identifies Himself with poor, suffering humanity !

In a German orphan home a place at the table was left vacant, and in the grace before meals the Lord Jesus was asked to come and take the vacant place. " Why does Jesus never come ? " asked a new orphan. " He may come to-day," was the reply. In the evening a poor, hungry, wandering child was heard crying outside. He was brought in and placed at the table in the vacant place. " That is not Jesus," said the orphan who had asked about His coming. " Forasmuch as ye have done it unto one of the least of these, ye have done it unto Me," was the reply of the master of the home.

We rejoice to think that in many, and in an increasing number, of the pulpits of our land the whole counsel of God on this subject is declared; yet we have no doubt that there are some, possibly a large number of those who profess and call themselves Christians, belonging to different Churches, who would object to this practical teaching, and would say that those who thus taught did not preach *the gospel*—the gospel as conceived by them having little or no concern with our duties to our fellow-men. When we have heard Christians in meetings for humiliation and prayer confess their sins, acknowledge that they did not "speak a word for the Master " when they might have done so, that they did not read the Bible as often as they might, that they did not use the means of grace as regularly or as devoutly as it was their privilege to do, we have wondered why they did not add that they had not relieved the distress of the poor and needy, that they had not treated more liberally those dependent upon them, that they had not taken a more active part in trying to promote the welfare of society.

Now no matter how exalted may be the teaching, or how spiritual the exercises in the house of God, the gospel of Christ is not fully preached if the duty of loving and serving man is not made as prominent as the great Master made it. Although having all possible sympathy with those who desire to deepen the spiritual life of our Churches, we sometimes cannot help thinking that if they would come up to the New Testament standard, they would try to broaden it as well.

CHAPTER XI.

LIBERTY, equality, fraternity,—these three words form the
motto of Socialism. Socialists extol liberty, and bitterly
complain of the slavery that they assert individualism
involves. They point to the fact that many workers have
no choice so far as the kind of work they will do is concerned, nor have they a choice of residence. They must
take whatever work is offered to them, and they must live
where they can conveniently attend to their work, or they
must starve. Thus are they slaves.

It must be admitted that many persons are in a condition in which their personal liberty is greatly circum-
scribed by the exigences of existence. Socialism, however,
would not mend matters. The tendency of legislative and
social movements is in favour of increased individual
liberty. Socialism, if established, would lead to its absolute
destruction.

The present industrial *régime* differs from Socialism as
the morning dawn differs from the evening twilight. At
present we are advancing, perhaps not very rapidly, but
yet most certainly, to the day of perfect individual, civil,

and religious liberty; under Socialism we should soon find ourselves in the dark night of unmitigated slavery. This, indeed, is one of the great evils of Socialism.

There is in humanity a deeply seated desire for individual liberty. Liberty is one of those things that the longer it is possessed the more highly is it appreciated. Even the born slave prizes freedom, but he who has once been free can never be a willing slave.

Men do not possess liberty in any high sense in which there is not liberty, "first in the inward domain of consciousness," that includes liberty of conscience, of thought and feeling, of opinion and sentiment; secondly, "liberty of tastes and pursuits, including the framing the plan of our life to suit our character"; thirdly, the liberty of combination for any purpose that does not involve harm to others.

Now Christianity secures our individual liberty by insisting on two fundamental principles which are necessarily destructive of interference with personal liberty by any power external to ourselves, either the authority of State or Church, or the power of public opinion. One principle is that every man is responsible to God, and should obey God rather than man. Writing to the Corinthians, St. Paul said, "But with me it is a very small thing that I should be judged of you, or of man's judgment. . . . He that judgeth me is the Lord." He also said, writing to the Romans, "So then each one of us shall give account of himself to God." This does not by any means imply that there ought not to be human legislatures and laws; but it does imply that, when this principle is adopted by those who make laws, they will not legislate on matters that ought to be left to each man to settle for himself.

Another principle that Christianity teaches is that every man has the right of private judgment. " Let each man be fully satisfied in his own mind," says St. Paul in the Epistle to the Romans. This principle teaches us not to force or punish men for their opinions, but to try to convince or persuade them.

These two principles of " individual responsibility to God " and the " individual right of private judgment " must lead to civil and religious liberty as a matter, not of favour, not even of Christian fraternity, but of right to every human being.

It may be said that Christianity only substitutes one slavery for another; that whilst it has a tendency to free man from slavery to man, it places him in a condition of slavery to God. St. Paul calls himself the slave of Jesus Christ. Now it may be argued the one slavery is as unworthy of man as the other, and as incompatible with true liberty.

To this objection we reply, that whilst regarding submission to God as the initial duty, there is in that submission no element incompatible with the truest freedom. If a man works out a proposition in Euclid, and comes to the conclusion, for example, that the three angles of a plane triangle are equal to two right angles, do we for a moment suppose that his intellect has yielded up any measure of its liberty ? On the contrary, we say that, in acting in accordance with the laws of its being, it has exercised itself in accordance with the highest conception of liberty, and that if it had come to the conclusion that the three angles of the plane triangle were equal to four right angles, it was not free, but in bondage to some corrupting influence.

So when there is on the part of man's intellectual or moral nature an act of submission to God,—who is the God of truth and of right,—there is in that act of submission an act of the truest liberty, because it is an act in full accordance with the laws that should control the soul. When man acts contrary to the will of God, then he is in bondage to some alien force. So true is it that, "if therefore the Son shall make you free, ye shall be free indeed."

Now we find that Christianity has abolished slavery. Whilst it is the case that no crusade against slavery was undertaken by the early Christian Church, yet as Christianity prevailed slavery was modified. That slaves had rights was acknowledged; they were protected by the laws, and ultimately slavery was abolished.

The author of *Gesta Christi* traces the influence of Christianity in the gradual abolition of slavery, which is practically first seen in the laws of Constantine, then more fully in the laws of Justinian, until we have in the ninth century the first formal command of the Church against slavery, in the words of St. Theodore of Stade : " Thou shalt possess no slave, neither for domestic service nor for the work of the fields; for man is made in the image of God."

" Whatever motives," says Mr. Brace, " Constantine himself may have had in his change of faith, the jurists who framed his legislation were evidently inspired and influenced by Christianity. In laws relating to slavery, we hear of 'being imbued with Christian discipline' as a reason for humanity; of emancipating in church with 'religious purpose,' and numerous other expressions which indicate the new forces working on the lawgivers. The 'day of the Lord' has become a day appropriate to emancipation and to a rest from all litigation; and emancipation in church has the same legal force with the formal emancipation of a Roman citizen. The official setting free of a slave became common as an act of piety or gratitude to God at recovery from illness, at the birth of a child, at death, or in wills. Many charters and epitaphs bore the expression of 'liberty for the benefit of the soul.'

"The Church early included a prayer in its liturgy 'for them that suffer in bitter bondage.' The burial inscriptions and pictures recently made known often show the masters standing before the Good Shepherd, with a band of their slaves, liberated at death, pleading for them at the last judgment. But scarcely any Christian inscription speaks of the dead as a 'slave' or 'freedman,' but only of the 'slave of Christ'; as if human slavery could not even be mentioned in the kingdom of God.

"A series of remarkable laws under Constantine showed the new spirit working upon legislation. In 312 A.D. a law was passed, declaring the poisoning of a slave, or the tearing of his body with the nails of a wild beast, or branding him, to be homicide. In 314, liberty was declared a right which could not be taken away; sixty years of captivity could not take from the freeborn the right of demanding liberty. In 316, Constantine writes to an archbishop: 'It has pleased me for a long time to establish that in the Christian Church masters can give liberty to their slaves, provided they do it in presence of all the assembled people and with the assistance of Christian priests, and provided that, in order to preserve the memory of the fact, some written document informs where they sign as parties or as witnesses.' In 321, he directs that ' he who under a religious feeling has given a just liberty to his slaves in the bosom of the Christian Church, will be thought to have made a gift of a right similar to Roman citizenship.' But this privilege is only granted to those who emancipate under the eyes of the priest. In 322, various laws defined methods by which persons whose liberty is assailed, even after sentence, may present new proofs of liberty and secure it."

Liberty is essential to the progress and development of the human race. If a man conforms to the customs of his day simply because they are customs, his doing so does not in any wise develop his own powers. In order to exercise his faculties of perception and judgment, he must make a choice. But if he blindly follows custom, he does not make any choice. He does not exercise the faculties employed in desiring and discerning that which is best. He has not "by reason of use his senses exercised to discern good and evil." He cannot "approve the things that are excellent," because he has not "proved the things that differ." Consequently his character is not developed, and it becomes inert and torpid instead of active and energetic. It is evident, then, that any system which does not give liberty to the human being hinders the development of the race; and because Christianity confers in many cases, and in every case favours, freedom, it has been and must ever be an important factor in promoting the well-being and progress of society.

In order that there may be progress there must be individuality of character. It is those persons who try experiments, and form new and higher ideals, who lead society into new and better ways. John Stuart Mill says: " A people, it appears, may be progressive for a certain length of time, and then stop. When does it stop? When it ceases to possess individuality." Individuality cannot flourish—it cannot even exist—except in an atmosphere of freedom. Without freedom human beings are as if they were turned off to order, according to one given pattern. Without freedom the human mind is " cabined, cribbed, confined."

So soon as society ceases to progress it commences to retrograde, as surely as man having reached the zenith of his powers begins to decline. The downward course may be carried on by slow and almost imperceptible degrees, but it has set in and, as a rule, cannot be averted. It can never be averted unless there is freedom which permits the play of recuperative forces, and with the development of individuality society may be rescued from destruction.

Hence under the influence of freedom the human race has attained a robustness of character and a degree of social development that it has never attained when individual liberty has been seriously curtailed. Consequently Christianity as the friend of liberty has also been the friend of the progress and the development of humanity. Socialism is destructive of individual liberty. Anarchism would not be so destructive of liberty as international Socialism ;

but anarchism means a return to barbarism, a statement that in another chapter we shall prove.

In a small self-governing area, producing all that is required by its inhabitants, with a limited trade and little communication with the outside world, there might be a fair amount of personal freedom, but it would be purchased at an enormous cost. Anything worth calling civilization can only be maintained by free intercourse with the world at large. On our breakfast tables there are the products of the uttermost parts of the earth. Civilization, with all its appliances of comfort, would be too high a price to pay for the measure of personal liberty afforded by communism. Therefore as we believe, with the large majority of Socialists, that the only possible form of Socialism is international Socialism, we shall not in this connexion any further consider communism.

Let us see, then, how liberty would fare under international Socialism. We suppose, for the sake of argument, that the form of Socialism known as collectivism has been established over the civilized world. It would be necessary now, in order to avoid the difficulty resulting from the numbers who would try to shirk their work under the public organization of labour, to provide a rigid system of inspection, and to be prepared for the prompt employment of force. It is evident that no strikes could be permitted, and that all must be kept to their work, or else the entire system would break down; for if it broke down at one point it must break down altogether. The necessary tendency of organized labour is to create a large class who would devote themselves to work at minute portions of manufacturing, and a small class who would control and organize. Few are possessed of the faculties requisite for organization on a large scale, and those who devote their powers to, say, making pin heads, filing the points of needles, or some other department in the almost infinite division of labour, would be incapable of organizing. Immense power would be thus placed in the hands of the few organizers. Let us see what they would have to do.

1. Settle what work each child should be trained up for doing, so that there might be the "direct adaptation" of the individual for his work.

2. Determine what shall be produced, and in what quantities.

3. Determine how long each man shall work.

4. Determine what amount of the common product each shall receive.

5. Determine what means shall be used to compel unwilling or indolent workers to do their due proportion of work.

These organizers, "omniarchs" as they have been called, would have power greater than any that has ever been possessed by the most absolute governments that have ever existed. Socialism, that would train every man for a certain work, that would appoint every man his place, that would apportion his wages and measure out his pleasures, would thus absolutely destroy individual liberty. So that those who now cry out against centralization and despotism would establish a monster centralization and a gigantic despotism beyond anything that does now or ever did exist.

We have hitherto supposed these "omniarchs" to be

fair, conscientious men ; but from what history teaches us
of human nature, no small body of men possessed of such
enormous powers, and not subject to the criticism of a free
and enlightened public opinion, would long continue pure.
Soon they would become corrupt and tyrannical; and
a more odious form of government would have been
established than that of the " wicked ten " in Venice, or
of the worst oligarchies of the ancient states of Greece.

Let those who favour Socialism remember that it can
only be established by stamping out individual liberty.
Freedom of demand is a first essential of freedom in
general. If the means of life and of culture were somehow allotted to each from without, and according to an
officially drawn up scheme, no one could live out his own
individuality, or develop himself according to his own
ideas ; the material basis of freedom would be lost. The
right to hold private property and individual liberty stand
or fall together.

The author of *Papacy, Socialism, and Democracy* says :
" That the intervention of public authority enfeebles private
initiative is a reproach to which, at all events, its interference is liable, and which is most important when
dealing with social matters. This alone would be alarm-
ing, for private initiative has at all times been the
mainspring of progress ; and to harass it or to paralyse
it by hampering it with laws and regulations which stay
or impede its work is to trammel the progress of industry
and wealth, and to delay improvement in the condition of
the masses."

Socialism, which, according to an eminent author,
has for its " Alpha and Omega the transformation of

private and competing capitals into a united collective
capital," by destroying private property destroys individual liberty. The new slavery would be worse than
the old, because more extensive. The degeneration of
the race would follow, and after a little time outraged
humanity would cast away its shackles—not, however,
without much suffering and loss. In a word, Christianity
is the friend of freedom and of humanity; Socialism is
nominally the friend of freedom, but really the friend of
slavery and the foe of freedom, and consequently of the
well-being, progress, and development of the human race.

In some cases the battle has been between a ruling
man or a ruling caste on one hand, and the mass of men
on the other. In some lands this struggle is over, and
a constitutional government has been established, under
which all are duly considered; in other lands this struggle
is still going on.

Then, again, in other cases the struggle is between a
majority disposed to be tyrannical and a minority. A
majority may be as tyrannical as a despot, and is likely
to be more so. A despot will frequently be led to
adopt moderate measures from personal fear. A majority
cannot temper its course from fear, for example, of
assassination, for there may not be any one who is
pre-eminently obnoxious to the minority. A despot may
have a sane moment, when he may reflect on the numbers
who do not agree with him. A large majority naturally
becomes impatient, and pleads, It is not possible that all
we can be wrong, and that "miserable," "despicable,"
"obstinate," etc., etc., minority right; away with them, they
must yield.

It is quite possible that there may be many a hard fought field before majorities learn these two lessons.

One is, that majorities may be wrong. This is a mere truism, but it is frequently overlooked — especially by majorities. If Christianity be true, as we firmly believe it is, then, so far as religion is concerned, the vast majority of men now living are wrong, for they are not Christians. History shows us that in no one period has the majority of the race been on the side of right and truth. "The world," says Carlyle, "has ever shown but little favour to its teachers. The prison, the poison chalice, and the cross are the market price it has offered for wisdom, the welcome with which it has met those who came to instruct and to purify it." "Which of the prophets did not your fathers persecute?" asked St. Stephen. To surrender our intellectual independence to a majority is just as bad, indeed probably is less defensible, than to surrender it to a pope.

The other and more important lesson that majorities have to learn, and one that they are even more prone to overlook, is that *minorities have rights with which majorities have no right to intermeddle.* This follows as a corollary from the principles of responsibility to God and right of private judgment already mentioned. There is no true liberty in a land in which the minority cannot act independently, so long as they do not by their action injure their neighbours, or unduly curtail their personal liberty.

Men have felt liberty so important that they have sacrificed everything for its sake. It has roused the enthusiasm of heroes and poets. It has nerved the patriot's arm.   Socialism is its sworn foe.   It means the absolute rule of the majority, and that rule absolute in all things.   It encroaches on every sphere.   It trenches on every interest.   It tramples on all independence.   It is fatal to liberty, and therefore fatal to the progress, welfare, and happiness of the human race.

CHAPTER XII.

IN uttering its watchwords, Socialism says "liberty" with
bated breath, it says "fraternity" with greater boldness,
but it lays special emphasis on "equality." "Inequality
is hateful to all but the highest," says one of the Fabian
essayists.

It is not for "equality of right" that they plead. That
is the equality recognised by the American constitution—
every man is free and equal *before the law*. It is not, however, the equality that Socialists demand.

Christianity teaches an equality of right. It requires
that no one shall be treated unjustly, either by private
individuals or by public functionaries; the ideal magistrate
does not bear the sword in vain, is "a terror to evil-doers,
but a praise to them that do well." It recognises the right
of every man to the ordering of his own life; but it does
not teach that all men are equal in intellectual or moral
faculties, or ought to be equal in position or in material
possessions.

Equality is not in accordance with the order and course
either of nature or of providence. If God had intended

10

equality to prevail in human society, He would have made human beings equal in the cradle. He has not done so.

Men are born with unequal physical powers. Some are born with the germs of positive disease in their systems, which will and must ultimately develop and cause their physical ruin. Consumption, cancer, gout, a strumous diathesis, are the terrible inheritance of many. Some are born with such delicate constitutions that no skill or care can ever produce vigorous health. Others have a fair average constitution; and a few have an iron frame, enormous strength that enables them to perform herculean feats. There have been men who could fell an ox with a single blow of their hand, or could bend a strong poker between their fingers as if it were a willow twig. They could endure extreme fatigue, undergo enormous toil, and for years seemed able to defy disease and death.

Whilst there are thus great differences in the original endowment of physical strength, there are even greater differences in the intellectual faculties that are distributed amongst the race. There are faculties given to some men that seem withheld entirely from others.

Then the same faculty is given to different men in different degrees. It is impossible to represent those differences, with any approach to accuracy, by figures. Suppose, however, that we take the figure one as representing the measure of the poetic faculty that the merest rhymester possesses, by what figure then shall we represent the poetic faculty of Homer, or Milton, or Shakespeare? If we knew the number of men who in all the ages had equal opportunities of culture with those poets, and then divided that number by the number of those that produced poetry equal to theirs, would the quotient be an approximate number to represent their poetic faculty ? If it would, then we should have to represent it by a number practically unknown to our arithmetic.

If we take the figure one as representing the average memory of a cultivated man, what figure shall we take as representing the memory of Cardinal Mezzofanti, who was familiar with sixty languages,—some of them composite and inflected as the English, and others uninflected and syllabic as the Chinese,—who could learn a grammar of a language by once reading it over, and did not know what it was to forget a word once heard or read ?   How can we express the difference between the mental faculties of Pascal, who as a child worked out correctly twenty propositions of the first book of Euclid, before he had seen a book on mathematics or had received any instruction in that science, and the faculties of the boy who, making as great an effort as he possibly can, aided by teachers and books, yet finds that the *pons asinorum* presents such an inscrutable mystery that he cannot get any farther in his study of Euclid.   The difference is simply inexpressible.   We may say that the faculties differ infinitely.   The asymptote may be extended to infinity, but it will never touch the hyperbola.   So there are minds, no matter how they are cultivated or how earnestly they strive, which can never accomplish work equal to that accomplished by other minds.

Do you doubt this ?   Can you write poetry ?   Try and equal Tennyson.   Can you paint ?   Try and equal Doré.   Can you compose music ?   Try and equal Handel or Wagner.   Now after trial, if you be the ordinary man and not the exceptional genius, you will confess that no exercise of the faculties you have will enable you to produce work equal to that produced by those who are differently endowed.

It is not, however, to be supposed that society is composed of only two classes, those who have remarkable mental endowments and those who have endowments few and small. There are the two classes, but between them there is a variety that cannot be tabulated. As it is true that no two human faces amongst the countless myriads of human faces were ever exactly alike, so it is likely that no two human souls ever possessed exactly the same faculties in exactly the same degree.

Now as men are not born physically equal nor intellectually equal, neither are they born morally equal. Of course we know that all men are born in sin, yet there is a different shade and a deeper dye. The physical constitution has a marked effect upon the moral character. A close student of the criminal remarks, " On this physical insensibility rests that moral insensibility, or psychical analgesia, which is the criminal's most fundamental characteristic."

" Benedikt, in 1879," writes Mr. Ellis, " published some interesting generalizations on the brains of criminals which he had examined. He found special frequency of confluent fissures; that is to say, according to his own description, if we imagine the fissures of the brains to be channels of water, a swimmer might with ease pass through all these channels. The question of confluent fissures had before this time attracted the attention of Broca, and his conclusions may probably still be accepted : ' One or more of these communications,' he said, ' do not prevent a brain from being at once very intelligent and very well balanced; but when they are numerous, and when they affect important parts, they indicate defective development. They are often seen in the small brains of the weak-minded and idiots, very frequently also in the brains of murderers, with this difference, that in the first case they are related to the smallness of the convolutions and of the brain generally; while in the second case they coincide with convolutions for the most part ample in size, and bear witness to irregularity in cerebral development.' Flesch studied the brains of fifty criminals, and found that every one presented some anomaly, sometimes of a remarkable character, as incomplete covering of cerebellum by cerebrum. He found two kinds of deviation common, one characterized by less richness of convolution than is found usually in ordinary brains, the other characterized by much greater richness of convolution than he had ever observed in normal brains. On the whole, we may agree with Hervé, that 'what the brains of criminals present, not characteristically, but in common with those of other individuals badly endowed, though by no means criminals, is a frequent totality of defective conditions from the point of view of their regular functions, and which renders them inferior.'"

A man who is born with an unstable nervous system will be therefore liable to tornadoes of passion. Just as we find that there are intellectual idiots, in whom the reasoning faculties are so small as to be barely discernible, so there are *moral idiots*, who have scarcely even an elementary conscience. They take naturally to crime, and have not the shrinking and aversion from it that are found in the normal mind.

By the mysterious laws of heredity there are lusts and passions congenital in many, so that we have the *instinctive criminal*, with a well-nigh irresistible impulse to crime. As in the tiger there is a latent love for blood, so in many there is a slumbering love of drink, which only needs the taste of it to arouse the appetite into a fatal wakefulness and vigour. "Who can escape the overwhelming past?" "The fathers have eaten sour grapes, and the children's teeth are set on edge."

On the other hand, there are men born with amiable dispositions, with great tenderness of conscience, with an earnest love of right, men with a moral nature responsive to all holy influences, who turn to what is good and true as the flower to the sun.

There are great differences between men morally. We cannot adequately formulate the difference between a John the Baptist, filled with the Holy Ghost from his mother's womb, and a Nero showing as a lad his cruelty and lust; between a Marcus Aurelius and a Cæsar Borgia; between a John Fletcher, who never knew what it was "not to fear God," and a girl of whom Mr. Ellis tells us, who, wanting some sweetmeats a little girl had, deliberately murdered the child to get them.

We do not mean to imply that either the natural goodness or wickedness of men destroys the freedom of the human will. Those naturally the worst, by the aid of divine grace, can do right, and those naturally the best are "free to fall." Yet it is easier for some to be good than it is for others, and it is easier for some to be vile than it is for others. In many cases there is a fierce struggle with evil of which those more happily constituted have no conception. In very homely phrase George White-field expressed a great practical truth when he said " that an ounce of grace would go as far with some as a pound with others." In forming our judgments of men morally we are always liable to error ; for whilst we may know what is done, we cannot tell " what is resisted."

Now there are certain combinations of qualities, physical, intellectual, and moral, which, as society is constituted, *must* bring some men to the front, and with equal cer-tainty must lead others to the back. By a natural law that cannot be evaded, iron will sink and cork will float in water ; so by the operation of laws as certain in their action, some men will be honoured and trusted, and others will not secure the respect or confidence of society. Take a man who is dull and stupid, and who is at the same time untruthful, it is not possible for him, when he is known, to stand on a level with the man who is intelligent and reliable. Society will and must, by its intelligent instinct of self-preservation and sense of justice, recognise the worth of the one and the worth-lessness of the other, and consequently will treat the one better than it does the other.

The idea of equality must break down, because it is not in accordance with the eternal verities. God has not made men equal by nature, and any artificial attempt to do so must end in disappointment and failure.

If it were possible to make all men equal in possession, position, reputation, and authority to-day, so long as they were not made intrinsically equal, their essential in-equality would assert itself before the rising of to-morrow's sun, and the relations of ruler and ruled, of teacher and taught, of borrower and lender, would reappear. The rash Esau, willing to sell his birthright for a mess of pottage, and the cool Jacob, ever ready to make a good bargain, would be found again. To try to make men equal artificially, until they are made equal naturally, is about as absurd as if men said, "We have two great lights in the heavens, the sun and moon, and from henceforth we decree that they are equal"; whilst their natural inequality remains just the same as before. So even if Socialism, with its dream of equality, were established, it would soon be overturned, and the inequalities in human society would speedily reappear.

Inequality has certain practical advantages connected with it. The objects of society are more conveniently accomplished by means of men with different faculties and aptitudes, than they could be by men who were all alike.

In a shipbuilding yard, or in a cabinetmaker's shop, there are various instruments, and many different sizes of each sort of instrument. As a rule, the more perfect the assortment of tools, the more rapidly the work will be done, and the work turned out will probably be better work than it would be if the appliances of production were less complete. If any person went into that yard or shop and insisted that all hammers and files and planes should be exactly equal, he would be told that each instrument had its use, that each one was fitted for its specific work, that there was a work the large hammer could do which could not be done so well by the small one, and a work the small hammer could do that could not be done so well by the large one.

So is it in carrying on the work of the world. Men

with various faculties and with various degrees of the various faculties are needed to work together for the common good. There are men with certain aptitudes and tastes, and having these they can with ease and pleasure to themselves perform important services to society, the doing of which would be almost intolerable to others.

It is necessary that we should have sailors ; our complex civilization could not be continued without their aid. Now we find men who have a love for a seafaring life ; they are more at home on the ocean than on the land ; they have a natural taste and aptitude for the life of a sailor. There are others for whom such a life would have no attraction. A life spent quietly in the country, or amid the vicissitudes and emulations of commerce, or in literary pursuits, or in scientific investigation, would gratify their taste.

Society needs men who will, not reluctantly, but cheerfully, adopt the various pursuits and callings which are necessary to the very existence of a civilized community. It is necessary that we should have men with such faculties that they will efficiently serve society in those different positions. Now we find men with "gifts differing," and hence there is an adaptation between the wants of society and the provision for these wants in the existence of men with different tastes and faculties. It is as evidently for the convenience of society that there should be variety in men, as that there should be variety amongst the tools in a workshop.

When Socialists cry out for equality, and say that men ought to be placed sometimes at one work and sometimes at another, or, at any rate, that all ought to be

regarded as equal, they entirely overlook the basis and
needs of society, and the fundamental facts of human
nature.   •

We cannot, indeed, imagine how the business of the
world could be carried on if equality, in any real sense,
were established.   Let us suppose that we have to work a
railway company—with the exception of an army, perhaps
the best example of organized labour—on this principle of
equality.   At every station every porter is equal to the
stationmaster, every stationmaster is equal to the traffic
manager.   The traffic manager is equal to the chairman of
the board of directors; at the same time he is not superior
to any porter at any one of the stations.   If this equality
be realized by all, no one who knows human nature can
suppose that discipline could be maintained for twenty-
four hours.   One man's opinion is just as good as another's.
"Why should I obey my equal?" says the porter, when
the stationmaster gives orders.   "Why should I obey
my equal?" says the stationmaster, when the traffic
manager gives directions.   Distracted counsels, plans,
and officers perpetually changing, unseemly conflicts
would inevitably ensue, and the fate of a house divided
against itself would fall upon that unhappy company,
whilst many disasters would occur to its unfortunate
passengers.

In order successfully to conduct any important organization, there must be some authority or authorities which,
having a wider vision and a knowledge of facts unknown
to others, must have the right to decide and to command;
whilst the others must have faith in the wisdom of the
controlling power, and be ready to obey.   Does any one

suppose that an army could be successfully led through a campaign unless the soldiers felt that it was

> Theirs not to make reply,
> Theirs not to reason why,
> Theirs but to do and die?

No complex organization could be worked on the principle of equality. Inequality is an ultimate and absolute fact in human nature; and any system which does not recognise this is not true to the facts of the case, and therefore is a system essentially unsound and impracticable.

The inequality existing in society has a moral purpose; it is a means for the moral training of the human race.

The idea of equality appeals to envy—the vice that Longfellow calls the vice of republics, and that John Stuart Mill calls the most anti-social of all the vices. Envy looks with an evil eye and a malignant heart on all superiority. It has played an important and a baleful part in the history of states and of individuals. It has led to repression, to slander, to conspiracy, to robbery, to murder, and to war. It led Cain to slay Abel, Saul to hunt David as a partridge upon the mountains, and the chief priests to deliver Christ into the hands of the Roman governor. It has often been a bar to progress, but it has never helped an individual to be happy or a state to be great.

This evil passion is the moral basis of Socialism. To soothe envy there must be equality. This pandering to it is vain. Fix the hand of your barometer at "set fair," yet the storm will come. Assert that all men are equal, yet the inequality that exists in human nature will manifest itself, and envy will rage. It were as wise to build a city over a slumbering volcano, as to erect a social system on envy as its moral basis.

Christianity recognises the inequality that exists in society, and teaches us how to deal with it.

Those who are brought into contact with their superiors are taught to have that charity which envieth not. Those who are brought into contact with their inferiors are taught to honour all men: not to honour a man because he is great or rich, but because he is a man, because he has, with his superior, a common immortality and a common Saviour. Those placed in influential positions ought to regard those placed under them as placed there by God, and as the necessary, even if humble, instruments in carrying out the divine purposes; and therefore as fellow servants, not to be treated with contempt, but with consideration and respect.

Those placed in subordinate positions ought to regard those in higher positions, not as enemies, not with envy, but as having important duties to perform, and as working together for the common good. Mutual dependence, mutual helpfulness, mutual consideration, and mutual respect, are the moral lessons that ought to be learned from the inequality that exists amongst men. That those lessons are not always learned is not the fault of any one class. All classes have been to blame. This, however, is certain, that as Christianity pervades society those lessons will be learned, hatred between the different classes will cease, rich and poor, high and low, will feel that they are all members one of another, and that whilst all the members have not the same office and are not equally honourable, yet that, united together in love, they will accept the statement of St. Paul when dealing with this very question, " That there should be no schism in the body ; but that the members should have the same care one for another."

Inequality makes society picturesque and interesting. Monotony is the most deadly enemy of enjoyment. One colour ever before our eyes, one vast plane our only landscape, one food with one taste and one flavour our only viand, one sound ever in our ears, would make life intolerable. The greatest agony of the Inquisition was the agony of monotony. Those who had studied the human frame well, so as to be able to torture it most exquisitely, believed that the regular dropping of water, at constant intervals, upon the same exposed part of the body, caused the most excruciating agony.

We naturally desire variety. Hard as it is sometimes found to be to love our fellow men, with all the interest and attraction that variety gives them, if all were so similar, that meeting our fellows would be like a perpetual looking in a mirror or listening to an echo, we should be ready to anathematize the entire race, and to welcome a monster, because he would provide a change.

The equality that Socialism loves, if once secured, would rob life of all interest. The dead level would soon become absolutely repulsive. The thought that by no energy could one procure a change into a higher level of life would take away the charm of existence, and men would ask then, with more reason than they have at present, " Is life worth living ? "

Christianity recognises the natural inequality of men which leads to inequality of condition. It speaks of those who have five talents, and two talents, and one talent. It tells us to "render to all their dues: tribute to whom tribute is due; custom to whom custom; fear to whom fear; honour to whom honour."

It is thus a system in harmony with the facts of human history. It is a system in accordance with the analogy and course of nature. There is thus a strong presumption established that Christianity and nature have a common Author.

Socialism is a system in opposition to the facts of human history, and not in accordance with the order and course of nature; and hence a strong presumption is established that Socialism and nature have not a common Author. Hence it follows that Socialism is not a system adapted to the constitution and necessities of our humanity, and consequently it is unworthy of our acceptance.

CHAPTER XIII.

The Principle of Fraternity—The Fraternity of Socialism—Fraternity without Fatherhood—Mr. John Burns, M.P., and the Russian Wolves—Is Christian Fraternity a Failure?—The Broad View —Practical Results of Christian Fraternity.

THE third of the famous watchwords of Socialism is "fraternity." It is in reality a principle of Christianity. We shall contrast the fraternity of Christianity with the fraternity of Socialism.

Socialism teaches fraternity without fatherhood. It tells men that they are brothers, but it gives no reason for their brotherhood except its own assertion. Christianity tells men that they are brothers, and gives the sufficient reason, because they have a Father in heaven. God is not the Father of one class of men considered either socially or morally. He is the Father of the spirits of all flesh. All souls are His. He is "our Father" who is in heaven. He is the perfect Father—that is, complete, universal in His beneficence—who "maketh His sun to rise on the evil and the good, and sendeth rain on the just and the unjust."

Here, indeed, is a reasonable ground for regarding our fellow men, even those of them deepest sunk in guilt and sorrow, those of them most alien to ourselves in thought and sympathy, as our brothers, because we are all the children of the one great Father. Socialism, which does not admit the fatherhood of God, has no solid ground for

teaching the brotherhood of man. The fraternity which
Socialism teaches is of a very narrow character. It does
teach fraternity amongst the proletariat, but it does not
extend it to the *bourgeoisie.* Of the rich and powerful it
speaks in terms of indifference or of hatred. Their spoliation, nay, their very destruction, it regards with equanimity.
A revolution in which much blood of the *bourgeoisie* is shed
is spoken of as a " mere incident," not even called a regret-
table incident.

According to the *London Quarterly Review* (April, 1893),
Mr. John Burns said : " The more the workers got, the
more they would demand. The driver of a sledge across
the Russian steppes was pursued by a pack of hungry
wolves. To appease the wolves the driver first tossed
them his own cap. But this was fruitless. He then threw
out his mantle. But the wolves followed fast as ever.
Then he gave up his provisions, which effected a momentary
diversion ; but the wolves were soon again by his side.
Then he sacrificed one child, then another, and last of all
his wife ; but the wolves, after devouring them, seeing the
driver and the horses still in front, kept up the pursuit.
In fine, when the horses are devoured, the driver, too, must
rejoin his family in the stomachs of the wolves. The
driver is capital, the possessors ; the wolves are the
Socialists ; the road across the steppes is the path of human
progress ; and the cap, the mantle, the children, and the
wife, abandoned one by one to the wolves, are the concessions made every day by the capitalists to the proletariat,
—the reforms to which they are compelled to assent, under
pain of being themselves devoured. And sooner or later,
unless they are careful, their turn will come. Little by

little we shall take all; as soon as we obtain one liberty we shall demand another. The wolves, the wolves, you know—the wolves behind the sledge."

' The fraternity of Socialism is a poor, partial, class affection,—a feeling, of course, higher than mere selfishness, but yet devoid of any element that can rightly be called noble or magnanimous. In striking contrast to this purely class feeling is the fraternity of Christianity. It is not limited by considerations of race or creed or position. The fraternity of Socialism seems mean and contemptible when we read the words of Christ: " Ye have heard that it was said, Thou shalt love thy neighbour, and hate thine enemy: but I say unto you, Love your enemies, and pray for them that persecute you; that ye may be sons of your Father which is in heaven."

It has been said that whilst this Christian fraternity is a magnificent conception, infinitely superior—as sunlight is to moonlight—to the fraternity of Socialism, yet Christianity has practically failed to remedy the evils of society.

To this we reply, that on any fair historical review it must be admitted that Christianity has done more for the benefit of the human race than any other system. It has abolished slavery, many cruel and licentious sports, wholesale infanticide, private war, the cruel treatment of prisoners, the neglect of the sick, the wounded, the orphan, the widow, and the poor. It has elevated the condition of women; it has promoted peace, commerce, literature, science, and art.

Much as it has done, it would have done more if it had not been hindered by the obstinacy of its enemies and by the mistakes and infirmities of its friends. Christians have

11

often taken a narrow view of what this principle of fraternity involves. Love to man should lead us to do good, not only on a small scale, but on a large scale; and the larger the scale the better, as we shall thereby accomplish the larger amount of good. Yet whilst doing good on the small scale has always been acknowledged as doing good, doing good on the large scale has often been looked on as not doing good at all, and even sometimes as doing what a Christian ought not to do. It has always been admitted that it is a good work to give bread to the hungry; but it has sometimes been overlooked that the man who helps to extend commerce may give bread to the hungry in the very best way—that is, by giving, not charity, but employment.

Suppose there are two men who have equal resources, mental and material. One of them spends his time in seeking out and relieving cases of distress; the other spends his time and means in, say, building a factory, and successfully conducting a large business. He becomes year after year a richer man. He also employs some hundreds of hands. They, in their turn, give employment to builders, who build houses for them, to tailors, farmers, milkmen, coal merchants, miners, and many others who help in supplying their bodily wants. They purchase tea and sugar, and thus help the trade of distant lands and the great shipping industry. At the end of ten years, the man who devoted himself to relieve distress has relieved many sad cases; but he is now a poorer man, and less able to help society than he was at the beginning of his career. During the ten years, the amount of good done by the factory owner has been far greater and more widespread than that done by the philanthropist. For one that has been relieved, twenty have been kept from distress by having employment furnished to them. Yet the Christian who skilfully conducts a large business is often regarded as if he were solely serving himself, and not serving his generation by the will of God. This is a most unfair judgment; for suppose all Christians devoted themselves to philanthropy, to the neglect of lawful business, widespread distress in Christian circles would soon result. We must not be supposed to teach that our energetic business man should not directly relieve distress as well as indirectly. The one he ought to do, and not leave the other undone.

It is everywhere admitted that it is a temporal good work to visit the sick. Those suffering physical pain, and unable to help themselves, have a claim on the sympathy and help of all men, and especially of Christians. It is well for us to notice in passing that care for the sick and efforts to alleviate pain are mainly the result of Christianity. Natural feeling had some influence, but until Christianity was introduced the sick were treated with considerable indifference. The very methods of cure in many cases were cruel and barbarous. It is the influence of Christianity that has led to the use of anæsthetics to deaden the pain of operations. The same influence has led to the discovery and use of medicines less nauseous and revolting than those used in former times. There were no hospitals in the centuries before Christ, and the first one was built at Rome in the fourth century of the Christian era under the direct influence of Christianity.

Now if a Christian devotes time and thought and energy

to the work of getting sanitary laws enacted, or put into operation, by which hundreds may be saved from the pains of sickness, and hundreds of families from the bitterness of bereavement, is he not doing good works—works worthy of the highest commendation ?

Again, if a Christian scientist performs experiments, and after much thought makes such discoveries as enable him to relieve or to mitigate the agonies of thousands, is he not as really doing good as if he spent his time in personally cooling the hot brow of fever or quenching its burning thirst ?

We do not plead that individual cases of distress are to be neglected, but we do earnestly plead for a recognition of work on the larger scale as being truly Christian work. We plead that the service of humanity should be recognised as the service of Christ. We plead that when a Christian devotes himself to commerce, or to science, or to legislation, or to art, his work which benefits his fellow men shall be regarded as Christian work; that the narrow interpretation of that phrase shall be discarded; that the distinction between secular and sacred shall not be accentuated, but that the Christian seeking to do the will of God shall be regarded as engaged in Christian work in his study, his laboratory, his warehouse, his studio, the civic council-chamber, or the House of Parliament. Our Lord tells us that the kingdom of heaven is as leaven " which a woman took, and hid in three measures of meal, till the whole was leavened." All life, all society, all thought should by the working of Christian men be leavened with the spirit of Christianity.

The Christian ought not to keep out of any sphere of

legitimate activity in which he may serve humanity for fear lest, morally speaking, the leaven should be unleavened by its contact with the meal, but should seek to bring every department of human life into captivity to the subjection of Christ. Nothing less than this is the obligation involved in the principle of Christian fraternity.

CHAPTER XIV.

Necessity for Revolution—Christianity sufficient to reform our Social Condition—It is opposed to the Causes of existing Evils—Idleness—Dishonesty—Drunkenness: Extent of; Financial Effects of; Vital Effects of—Alcohol and the Brain—"O Israel, thou hast destroyed thyself."

SOCIALISTS tell us that the vast amount of misery at present existing in society is the result of our vicious social system, and that in order to promote the well-being and happiness of society in general, the present individualistic system should be overturned, and a collectivist system established in its stead.

In opposition to this, our contention is that the great bulk of the wretchedness that is admittedly existent in society is the result, not of a faulty social system, but of so many human beings not ordering their lives in accordance with the precepts of Christianity. The suffering is to a very large degree self-inflicted; and not our social system, but human beings themselves, are to blame for causing their own troubles.

It often seems to be taken for granted that, when persons suffer, some one or other ought somehow or other to remove the suffering, and that society, or at least some portion of it, is to blame, and ought to be denounced because this suffering is allowed to continue. In a vast number of cases society is not to blame; the suffering is a righteous penalty, and should be allowed to continue until there is wrought an improvement in the sufferer. We ask, is there any good reason why men should not suffer when by their own sin and folly they have pursued a course of life which must and ought to bring suffering upon them?

The proposition we shall endeavour to establish is, that the precepts of Christianity duly observed would prevent a vast proportion of the evils that at present afflict our social life.

Idleness is one reason why many are in a state of destitution. They are not afraid to steal, nor ashamed to beg, but they are determined, if possible, not to work. They are ingenious in writing begging letters, and in devising means to play upon the sympathies of the benevolent. In carrying out their plans they show no little tact and perseverance. So thoroughly do they dislike honest work, that when compelled by sheer necessity to work, they will shirk their tasks, and do as little as possible ; and the little they do is ill done. If they can get wife or child to work for them, or to do worse, they will enjoy themselves by loafing about the street corners and the public-house.

Mr. Charles Booth says: "Unwillingness to work is closely connected with self-indulgence in other ways, and there is no known cure except the pressure of 'neither shall he eat.' Men who never work when it can be avoided, if without property, usually drift into pauperism, unless they have relations to sponge upon, or a wife ready to work for them. It is this extreme and most readily recognised form of laziness which usually appears as causing pauperism ; but another form of the same trouble is to be found with those who are unwilling to work regularly.

"The irregularity of waterside work reacts on the character and habits of the men who do it, and on their circumstances, as it becomes the custom for their wives to ‘ earn the rent ’ as a regular thing, and to feed themselves and their children when the man gets no work for a length of time. It may be necessity : a man may take all the work he can get, and still work very irregularly ; but there are others who are either constitutionally lazy, or with whom the habit has become engrained, who do not care to work more than three or four days a week. Nor would more money come to the home if they earned it. If such men make more they drink more. Laziness of this type is an important cause of poverty, and hence of pauperism sooner or later."

Idleness is a powerful factor in bringing many down to a position lower than that which they formerly occupied. Men carrying on business have found that business " becoming small by degrees and beautifully less," simply because it was not attended to. Men have gone down from one situation to another, each succeeding one of less importance and smaller income, because they did their work negligently. Solomon said :

> I went by the field of the slothful,
> And by the vineyard of the man void of understanding ;
> And, lo, it was all grown over with thorns,
> The face thereof was covered with nettles,
> And the stone wall thereof was broken down.
> Then I beheld, and considered well :
> I saw, and received instruction.
> Yet a little sleep, a little slumber,
> A little folding of the hands to sleep :
> So shall thy poverty come as a robber ;
> And thy want as an armed man.

Christianity condemns indolence. The Christian ought to be fervent in spirit, but he ought also to be diligent in business. So far from giving any encouragement to idleness, St. Paul lays down a rule that many would find bearing hardly upon them if it were universally enforced, "If any man will not work, neither shall he eat." Our Lord selects the unprofitable servant as one specially deserving of condemnation, and in the judgment pronounced upon him displays no sympathy with the slothful, but apparently implies that wickedness and slothfulness generally go together: "Thou wicked and slothful servant." In the rules of the Methodist Society Mr. Wesley says, for the guidance of his followers: "Giving all diligence and frugality, that the gospel be not blamed."

It is most unreasonable for Socialists to blame our social system for the ills that the idle man brings upon himself. It is not right that some kind-hearted philanthropists should join in this cry. Why should not the idle suffer? The law by which they do so is "just and good." It is for the advantage of society and of the individual himself that indolence should involve suffering.

A good deal of the wretchedness existing in society is produced by dishonesty. Thrifty persons save out of their hard-earned incomes sufficient to keep them independent in sickness or in old age, or it may be they save what will enable them to give their children a fair start in life. A widow is left with a small sum of money that with economy will be just sufficient to keep her from indigence. Those persons put their little capital into a building society, or into some business recommended to them. For a time those institutions seem not only safe, but prosperous. Some of the officials, however, it may be some of the directors, have expensive tastes. They indulge in costly luxuries, in magnificent and well - appointed mansions, in steam yachts, in a stud of racehorses, in a seat in Parliament. In order to meet their expenditure they purloin the funds committed to their care. In order to cover this they issue false reports, and make false statements at the company's annual meeting. But a thing of this sort cannot go on for ever. So the crash comes. Then there is a commercial scandal, a nine days' wonder, a flight into some country with which there is no extradition treaty, and hundreds of honest, industrious people are plunged into poverty.

The great suffering thus caused is not the result of our social system, but of flagrant violation of the precepts of Christianity. But is no blame at all to be attached to society for all this suffering ? We readily admit that society may be blamed to a certain extent, because the laws are not sufficiently stringent regarding the sacredness of property. Our laws require to be strengthened in the exactly opposite direction to that aimed at by Socialism. It is quite true that if a man steals a turnip or half-a-crown, he can be speedily and effectively dealt with. But there is this anomaly about our laws, that whilst its meshes prevent the escape of the little fish, they do not always retain the big fish, which is just the reverse of what ought to be.

We want our laws so improved that not only shall the man who by the simple and comparatively straightforward method of picking his neighbour's pocket, or of breaking into his neighbour's house, has violated the law, be visited with condign punishment, but that the more skilful and less straightforward thief, who can evade the law, yet on the Stock Exchange, or in the directors' board-room, in the high places of the commercial world, takes from others thousands and hundreds of thousands of pounds, shall be punished also. If our laws were made as stringent as they ought to be, and—if the present tendency, accelerated by recent revelations both in this country and in France, continue—as they soon will be, many in high positions then would be found, not as local magnates, or as legislators, or as leaders of fashion, but serving their term in the humble but healthy occupation of convicts in the prisons of our land.

Dishonesty causes distress, not only by its frauds upon the honest, but by its effect upon the dishonest man himself. There are many who are industrious, have a good address, and tact and business knowledge, and yet do not succeed, because they cannot be trusted. They are the men sometimes spoken of as "too clever by half." Without faith in one another society would be a rope of sand. The self-preserving instinct of society perceives this. Hence when once a man is known not to be honest, society discards him; and when a dishonest man brings himself to poverty and rags, he ought not to blame society, but himself. Christianity erects a high standard. It tells men not merely to be truthful, but to be trustworthy, "to show all good fidelity"; to act at all times under the obligations imposed, not merely by the letter, but by the spirit of the law. It commends him "who sweareth to his own hurt, and changeth not." The most inveterate sceptic must acknowledge the practical value of Christian probity. If employers and employed, if buyers and sellers, acted on Christian principles, disputes would be few, losses would be diminished, business would flourish, and the different classes would live in mutual confidence and harmony.

Another cause of many of our social evils is the prevalence of drunkenness. The extent to which drunkenness prevails demands our attention. The number of arrests made by the police is some indication. In one year it is stated that one person in every thirty was arrested in Liverpool, and one in thirty-eight in Manchester. In New York nearly fifty thousand arrests are annually made. Last year, in the city of Dublin, one person in twenty-four was arrested. These figures indicate the extent of drunkenness, but do not actually express it, because we may safely say that for every one arrested many get drunk who are not arrested, because they get drunk at home, or when intoxicated they keep quiet, or are kept quiet by their friends.

The number of public-houses is also some indication of the extent of this evil. In England there are nearly two hundred thousand houses engaged in the liquor traffic. In some parts of London there is one public-house for every thirty-nine other houses, and in some parts of Dublin there is one for every twenty-five. It has been calculated that the public-houses of Dublin, if placed side by side, and allowed a frontage of seven yards each, would form a street five miles long. Last year £140,866,262 was spent on intoxicating liquors in Great Britain. In Dublin the expenditure averaged ten thousand pounds a week; in Ireland, about eleven millions a year, being somewhat more than the entire rental of the country. The income of all the Christian Churches of the United Kingdom for

all purposes of maintenance and extension probably does
not exceed eighteen millions annually. Therefore the nation
spends on drink nearly eight times as much as it does on
religion ; or, to put it in another form, it gives to Bacchus
one pound for every half-crown it gives to Christ.

It may be supposed that a large portion of these vast
sums goes into the pocket of the working-man ; but such
is not the case. It has been calculated that if you spend
twenty shillings on any of the ordinary articles of commerce, such as clothes, food, books, etc., from six to eighteen
shillings go to the worker ; but in the case of drink not
more than one shilling will go to him.

Mr. Lewis states that in Scotland there are one hundred
and eighteen distilleries, employing altogether about six
hundred men ; but that if this same money were spent on
general good, more than forty-six thousand men would be
employed at thirty shillings a week.

A large establishment in Ireland, engaged in the manufacture of an alcoholic beverage, has a yearly turn over—
less duty paid—of about two millions. Of this large sum
only one hundred thousand pounds are paid as wages.
That is, five per cent of the turn over goes to labour. In
another establishment in Ireland engaged in the general
printing trade, thirty-three per cent goes to labour. Now
if a similar percentage went to labour in the first case, the
large sum of over six hundred thousand pounds would be
paid as wages.

Taking all businesses engaged in the manufacture of
alcoholic beverages, it may be fairly stated that not more
than five per cent of their turn over goes to labour ; of
other businesses, it may be taken for granted that from

twenty to thirty per cent of the turn over goes to labour. Thus other businesses can employ from four to six times as many, in proportion to the business done, as the manufacture of strong drink can, and pay them equally well. It is thus very evident that if the drink traffic ceased, and the capital employed in it turned to other trades, the increased proportion going to labour would immediately put an end to the difficult question of the unemployed. There would be such an immediate demand for labour, that every worker's wages would rise, and every one willing to work could get work to do.

The liquor traffic, then, benefits society at large less than any other business. This, however, does not adequately show the evil that results from it. We must consider that drunkenness causes much crime, disease, death, and insanity.

, Crime is very costly. In order that it may be detected, convicted, and punished, a large array of policemen, magistrates, barristers, judges, prisons, and prison officers must be maintained. Their support, amounting to millions annually, forms an enormous drain on the resources of the country.

It must not be supposed that if there were no drunkenness, there would be no crime. Sobriety does not bring every other virtue along with it. But it gives them a better chance of growing. If, however, there were no drunkenness, there would be far less crime. Drunkenness directly leads to crime, because it stimulates the passions, weakens the will, deadens the conscience, and obscures the judgment. Can it then be a matter of wonder that under its influence crimes are committed, and committed by

men who, if sober, would be orderly and law-abiding ?
Judge Bovil said : " Nine-tenths of the cases that have come
before me have been caused by strong drink." The late
Baron Dowse said that drink was at the bottom of almost
every crime committed in Dublin. Many judges have
corroborated what Judge Paterson said to the grand jury
at Norwich : " But for this drink, you and I should
have nothing to do." Drunkenness is a cause of disease
and death. Many diseases are caused by it directly.
Heart disease, apoplexy, and paralysis follow in its train.
At the Social Science Congress in Belfast, Dr. M'Ghee said
that four cases of disease out of five were caused by strong
drink. Many diseases are also caused by it indirectly ;
because drunkenness enfeebles the constitution, and renders
it less able to resist the germs of infection or other dangerous elements that are so often found in the water we
drink or in the air we breathe. The drunkard attacked
by fever, or almost any disease, has a far smaller chance of
recovery than the sober man. Even in those cases in which
it may be necessary to use alcoholic stimulants, the system
of the drunkard has become so accustomed to them, that
he does not get from them the same advantage as the sober
man. See how expensive a vice drunkenness is ! or may
we not rather call it a crime ? In addition to all that has
been mentioned before, we must add the loss of time resulting from the various diseases induced by it, and the doctors,
nurses, hospitals, and apothecaries that are consequently
employed. To the deaths from sickness we must add those
from accident and violence, of which drunkenness provides
an unfailing supply. The coroner for West Middlesex
stated that out of fifteen hundred inquests held by him,

nine hundred were caused by drink. Dr. Norman Kerr says: "A few years ago I instituted an enquiry to expose the falsity of the statement that sixty thousand drunkards died every year in the United Kingdom. I had not long pursued my enquiry before it was made clear to me that there was very little exaggeration in the statement, and at the Social Science Congress I was compelled to admit that at least one hundred and twenty thousand annually lost their lives through alcoholic excess."

We must also remember that drunkenness causes insanity. A proportion, variously estimated, but certainly considerable, of both idiots and lunatics are mental wrecks, either because of their own drunkenness or that of their parents. Alcohol is a brain poison. Dr. Ringrose Atkins says: "One of the most noticeable changes which occurs is the great increase in the number of the little seed-like bodies which are present in small numbers in the healthy brain. They now appear in such numbers as oftentimes to conceal or obliterate the normal structures of the bloodvessels, and obstruct its channel, thus depriving that portion of the brain of its nutrient supply. This condition is observed in the vessels of the pia mater, as well as in those penetrating the brain itself; and the latter membrane is seen dotted thick with these little seed-like bodies. It also becomes thickened, and loses its delicate translucency, appearing the colour of milk in patches and blotches, and it becomes glued, as it were, to the surface of the brain, tearing the latter when an attempt is made to strip it off the convolutions. These changes in the bloodvessels of the brain and its membranes occur also in those of the skin of the face especially, which become visible in the dull purplish hue and generally congested appearance of the chronic alcoholic.

"Following the structural changes in the bloodvessels come changes of a like character in the brain cells, the larger pear-shaped ones, which are found in the deeper layers of the cortex, being those chiefly affected. In the earlier stages they may become dotted over with the little seed-like bodies above mentioned, or these latter may actually penetrate their substance. Later on this substance becomes altered in appearance, masses of yellow granules taking the place of the normal structure. Then the delicate prolongations uniting cell with cell and with the nerve fibrils, which transmit their impulses downwards, become affected; they become granular, and finally break off and disappear, so that the vast network of cells, in health associated for co-operative work, becomes dissociated, and powerless in consequence, the result being, at first, a want of harmony in all mental, motor, and sensory activities, and finally the diminution, or, in advanced cases, the abrogation of these activities—in insanity and paralysis. A further change of a remarkable kind also occurs throughout the thickness of the cortex, especially in its outer layers; new cells are formed, which have no connexion with the manifestation of functional activity, but which have, on the contrary, the power of consuming, so to speak, the normal elements. These are called scavenger cells, as their province seems to be to sweep away the remains of the ordinary cells which are breaking down and becoming destroyed. A glance through the microscope at a section of a healthy brain, and then at a section from one thus altered under the influence of alcohol, is most interesting and instructive.

12

It is like looking at a stately ship with masts and ropes and sails in perfect condition and working order, and then beholding the same ship stranded upon the shore, a shattered wreck, bereft of all that made it beautiful and perfect."

The brain is the organ of the mind, and when it is injured the power to think rightly is lost. *Furor brevis mania est*, is an old proverb. It may be said with perfect truth of every bout of drunkenness that it is a brief mania, and these brief manias often lead to the complete extinction of the light of reason in the drunkard's soul. Other causes of insanity are rendered operative by the additional stimulus of drunkenness. The loss or disappointment that the sober brain can endure is often too much for the one weakened or deranged by drink.

Here, then, again we have drunkenness taking men and women out of the ranks of producers and putting them in the rank of consumers only. The insane cannot be left to starve and die. Asylums must be provided for them; doctors, matrons, and nurses must minister to their necessities, and keep them from injuring themselves or others. Thus, instead of helping to bear the common burden, those victims of their own vile habit become an additional burden on those who, without them, have quite enough to bear.

Not only is drunkenness such a serious drain on the resources of the present, but it mortgages those of the future. By the laws of heredity many of the children of drunkards are born with a well-nigh irresistible appetite for strong drink. They are instinctive drunkards. They have a keener appetite for strong drink than for the natural aliment of childhood. In Dublin, a short time ago, a boy only seven years of age died of *delirium tremens*. Just as we have received from the past a terrible legacy in the shape of a mass of perverted humanity, even so a similar legacy, let us hope of smaller dimensions, the future will receive from us.

There is another point of view from which we must look at this question—that of individual and family economics. Money spent on drink is not laid out to the best advantage. Suppose the case of a family earning wages so low that, with the wisest economy, they are barely able to keep themselves out of debt, and in what is regarded as decency in their class. Now if ten per cent of their wages—and ten per cent would be regarded as an exceedingly moderate amount—are spent on strong drink, there must be a certain diminution of comfort. Nothing can be given in charity, and nothing can be saved for the future. There must be a consequent decay of independence and loss of self-respect. The case will be much worse if twenty-five per cent of the wages are spent on drink. But if, as is the case with multitudes of those who drink freely, sixty per cent of the wages are spent on drink, then there inevitably follow squalor, insufficient nourishment, so far as the children are concerned, at any rate, causing serious injury to their health. The decencies of life in apparel and domestic furniture are not observed, the home life becomes a mere animal matter of herding together for shelter and food, with frequent and violent quarrels, and vicious or criminal means are resorted to in order that the appetites may be gratified.

Just imagine the outcry that would be raised, and justly raised, and what a strike would follow, if it were proposed to take ten, or twenty-five, or sixty per cent off workmen's wages! Yet this is what very many do to themselves. In fact, they do worse. The men, and especially their families, would be better off, if the deductions in the wages were retained by the employers, rather than given to the publicans. The moral effects of drunkenness would be avoided. The injury to health would not result. The fightings, quarrellings, and brawlings would not be induced. Far better would it be if the money were cast into the depths of the sea rather than into the publican's till.

In his work on *Pauperism*, Mr. Charles Booth has collected a large array of facts bearing on that subject. A study of those facts proves that by far the largest portion of pauperism is the result of causes that are moral and preventible. It is not the necessary outcome of the social system under which we live. It is not a stern fate that is against us. Our destiny is in our own hands. We select a few cases that are fair specimens of the large number contained in his book.

" A shoemaker. Single. Age thirty-three. Lazy drunkard. On more than one occasion pretended to commit suicide. Frequently in insane wards when suffering from *delirium tremens.*

"Widower. Age seventy-one. Many years ago kept a first-class hotel. Became absolutely destitute through drink.

" Shoemaker. Age seventy. Brought to ruin by drink. Could not work now ; but said that he always drank when he got work.

" Compositor. Age forty-seven. Went mad through drink. Was editor and proprietor of a paper in an eastern county, and doing very well indeed. Had two sons who would have supported him if he would have kept from drink.

" Single man. Labourer. Age thirty-eight. Chargeable many years; could get his own living, but too lazy to work.

" John Hunt. Age sixty-eight. Had been a custom-house officer for twenty-seven years, but had been dismissed for drunkenness, he said. It turned out afterwards that the actual cause of dismissal was larceny."

We have, then, three branches of a upas tree—idleness, dishonesty, drunkenness. This tree ramifies throughout our land—in city, town, and village—no part of the United Kingdom, no part of the civilized or uncivilized world, is free from it. Under its baleful shadow are to be found wretchedness in rags, physical suffering, mental imbecility, the agony of those detected in criminal courses, the shame of their friends, the bitterness of bereavement, blighted hopes, shattered reputations, "mourning, lamentation, and woe." Yet many put all the blame for this state of things on our social system, the administration of the government, our defective legislation. It is so pleasant to be able to blame other people and not oneself; it is so agreeable to confess the sins of others rather than our own! But if we would be honest, we must say to many of those who suffer, in the language of the prophet of old: "O Israel, thou hast destroyed thyself." You, indeed, by your own selfish indulgence, by your sin and folly, by your very own act and deed, have plunged yourselves and your families into degradation, wretchedness, and want. Blame not our social system; blame yourselves.

Now suppose that men would do what Christianity enforces, that they would live godly, righteous, and sober lives, what a change would result! Trade would revive, wages would increase, unnecessary expenditure would be cut off, and immediately vastly increased means of enjoyment would be placed under the control of the working classes. Better food, better clothing, better houses, and better furniture would all be available.

We contend that Socialism is wrong in charging all our social evils on the existing social system ; and that under this system Christianity is able to show us how to live lives elevated, contented, and useful, and gives us principles which, if accepted and acted upon, would remove every evil, and lead to such laws and adjustments as would make society as perfect as it could be made in this world.

Not another gospel, but to act upon the one we have, intelligent reform not destruction, evolution not revolution, is what we need. Christianity has sufficient forces to restore, and to bring to its highest development, our fallen humanity.

CHAPTER XV.

MR. GEORGE (as we have already seen, p. 109) states that the object of his enquiry is "the law which associates poverty with progress, and increases want with advancing wealth." He assumes and asserts that under the present *régime* the rich are growing richer, and the poor poorer. This statement is accepted by Socialists as expressing an undoubted truth. It is repeated in speeches and pamphlets and newspaper articles day by day. It is so often asserted, and so ready are a large number to believe what is frequently asserted, that many would as soon think of questioning an axiom—that the whole is greater than its part, for example—as they would of questioning the truth of this perpetually repeated assertion. Elaborate arguments are submitted to show why it is so, and why, under existing economic arrangements, it ever must be so.

When king Charles II. asked the Royal Society his celebrated question, "Why does not a dead fish add to the weight of a vessel of water, though a living one does?" he received a great many answers that had a profoundly philosophic sound.

But those philosophers did not examine into the truth of their data, and hence they have so often served as a warn- . ing, showing us that, before we give a reason for a supposed phenomenon, we ought to make sure of our facts. Consequently we propose to enquire, Is it true that at present the rich are ever growing richer, and that the poor are becoming poorer? We shall take the question exactly as it is stated by Mr. George himself.

"I mean," he says, "that the tendency of what we call material progress is in nowise to improve the condition of the lowest class in the essentials of healthy, happy human life. Nay more, that it is to still further depress the condition of the lowest class. The new forces, elevating in their nature though they may be, do not act upon the social fabric from underneath, as was for a long time hoped and believed, but strike it at a point intermediate between top and bottom. It is as though an immense wedge were being forced, not underneath society, but through society. Those who are above the point of separation are elevated, but those who are below are crushed down."

If this were so, it would evidently mean that there has been a steady decline in the rate of wages. On this subject we shall take as our authority Dr. Giffen. His pamphlet, *The Progress of the Working Classes in the last Half Century*, is spoken of by Mr. Gladstone as being "probably, in form and substance, the best answer to George." In it we learn that there has not been a steady decrease, but a steady increase in the rate of wages, and that not in one trade alone, but in all trades. Dr. Giffen says: "Thus in all cases where I have found it possible, from the apparent similarity of the work, to make a comparison, there is an enormous apparent rise in money wages, ranging from twenty, and in most cases from fifty, to one hundred per cent, and in one or two instances more than one hundred . per cent. This understates, I believe, the real extent of the change."

Agricultural labourers have not been excluded from their share in this general improvement. He says " that whilst the records of the Board of Trade do not include anything relating to the agricultural labourer, but from independent sources—I would refer especially to the Reports of the recent Royal Agricultural Commission—we may perceive how universal the rise in the wages of agricultural labourers has been, and how universal, at any rate, is the complaint that more money is paid for less work. Sir James Caird, in his *Landed Interest*, puts the rise at sixty per cent as compared with the period just before the repeal of the Corn Laws; and there is much other evidence to the same effect."

This increase in the rate of wages, it must be observed, is not given because there has been an increase in the hours of labour; on the contrary, whilst wages have increased, the hours of labour have diminished.

" The next point," says Dr. Giffen, " to which attention must be drawn is the shortening of the hours of labour which has taken place. While the money wages have increased, as we have seen, the hours of labour have diminished. It is difficult to estimate what the extent of this diminution has been ; but, collecting one or two scattered notices, I should be inclined to say very nearly twenty per cent. There has been at least this reduction in the textile, engineering, and house-building trades. The work-

man gets from fifty to one hundred per cent more money
for twenty per cent less work; in round figures, he has
gained from seventy to one hundred and twenty per cent in
fifty years in money return."

But whilst the rate of wages has increased and the
hours of labour have diminished, another important matter
requires to be considered before we can determine that the
actual condition of workers has improved, and that is the
purchasing power of money. If a labourer now gets two
pounds whereas formerly he got but one pound, yet if
formerly he could get more for his one pound than he can
now get for his two, it is evident that he is worse off, and
not better off, than formerly.

It is admitted that there has been a rise in butcher
meat and in house rent; we must therefore enquire, Will
the same amount of money get more or less of the other
necessaries of life now than some years ago?

In answer to this question Dr. Giffen states: " What
we have to consider, then, is, that fifty years ago the
working-man with wages, on the average, about half, or
not much more than half, what they are now, had at times
to contend with a fluctuation in the price of bread which
implied sheer starvation. Periodic starvation was, in fact,
the condition of the masses of working-men throughout
the kingdom fifty years ago, and the references to the
subject in the economic literature of the time are most
instructive. M. Quetelet, in his well-known great book,
points to the obvious connexion between the high price
of bread following the bad harvest of 1816 and the
excessive rate of mortality which followed. To this day
you will find tables in the Registrar-general's returns which

descend from a time when a distinct connexion between these high prices of bread and excessive rates of mortality was traced.

"It may be stated broadly, however, that while sugar and such articles have declined largely in price, and while clothing is also cheaper, the only article interesting the workman much which has increased in price is meat, the increase here being considerable. The 'only,' it may be supposed, covers a great deal. The truth is, however, that meat fifty years ago was not an article of the workman's diet, as it has since become. He had little more concern with its price than with the price of diamonds. The kind of meat which was mainly accessible to the workman fifty years ago, *viz.* bacon, has not, it will be seen, increased sensibly in price."

We must consider a little more fully the question of house rent, because it might be supposed that the rise in it counterbalances, or more than counterbalances, the fall in the price of general commodities. This is not the case. The rise in house rent, when deducted from the fall in articles in common use, leaves a balance in favour of the workman.

Suppose, as Dr. Giffen puts it, that fifty years ago a workman earned one pound a week, and that his house rent was five shillings a week. Let us suppose that now he earns two pounds a week, and that his house rent has increased by one hundred and fifty per cent, that is, from five shillings a week to twelve shillings and sixpence; yet that would leave him for other purposes twenty-seven shillings and sixpence as against fifteen shillings fifty years ago, and then each one of these twenty-seven shillings has a higher purchasing power of the necessaries of life than each shilling of the fifteen had. Consequently, notwithstanding the rise in house rent, which we have taken as one hundred and fifty per cent,—a higher figure than is warranted by the actual facts,—the workman is decidedly better off than he was fifty years ago.

It ought also to be remembered, that whilst a higher rent is charged, the houses now inhabited by working-men are vastly better than they were half a century ago. They are better built, have larger apartments, more light, better ventilation, better sanitary arrangements, and very many more conveniences and labour-saving appliances. At the higher rent the present houses are very much better value than the former ones were at the lower rent. When we consider to what a large extent the health and comfort, as well as the morals, of a family depend upon the house it dwells in, and contrast the workmen's houses of the present with those of the past, we must admit that in this respect, at any rate, the former days were not better than these.

If the rich were growing richer, and the poor poorer, the inevitable result would be an increased death-rate. The pressure of poverty always does and always must increase the death-rate. Less care and fewer comforts are then the lot of the young, the aged, the infirm, and the sick; therefore a larger proportion of them die than in those happier times when the needed care and comforts can be more freely given.

Instead, however, of an increased death-rate, we find that, owing to improvements in sanitation, to an increased supply of better food, and more healthful clothing, we have a considerably decreased death-rate.

Mr. Humphreys, in a paper on "The Recent Decline in the English Death-Rate," published in the *Statistical Society's Journal* (vol. xlvi.), shows conclusively that the death-rate is decreasing and the average of life increasing; and that this improvement is not amongst a select class only, but that it is a general improvement amongst the masses of the population.

Again, if it were true that the rich were growing richer and the poor becoming poorer, there would be an increase of pauperism. Of the poor, those in the margin between those able to maintain themselves and paupers would be pressed into the ranks of the pauper class, with a rapidity proportioned to the increased pressure of poverty.

Dr. Giffen says : "As regards pauperism, here the figures are so imperfect that we cannot go back quite fifty years. It is matter of history, however, that pauperism was nearly breaking down the country half a century ago. The expenditure on poor relief early in the century and down to 1830-31 was nearly as great at times as it is now. With half the population in the country that there now is, the burden of the poor was the same. Since 1849, however, we have continuous figures, and from these we show that, with a constantly increasing population, there is an absolute decline in the amount of pauperism. The earliest and latest figures are—

	1849.	1891.
England and Wales . .	934,000	780,457
Scotland . . .	122,000	86,835
Ireland . . .	620,000	107,129
United Kingdom .	1,676,000	974,421

Thus in each of the three divisions of the United Kingdom there is a material decline, and most of all in Ireland,
the magnitude of the decline there being no doubt due to
the fact that the figures are for a period just after the great
famine."

So eminent an authority as Mr. Froude has recently
said: "Even, however, in the outward essentials of food
and clothing and housing, it is not certain that the mass of
mankind in the present generation are better off than their
forefathers. Workmen and workmen's families have still a
hard time of it. Nor do I know that between them and
what are called the upper classes the feeling is better than
it used to be. I do not believe that the condition of the
people in mediæval Europe was as miserable as is pretended.
I do not believe that the distribution of the necessaries of
life was as unequal as it is at present. If the tenant lived
hard, the lord had little luxury. Earls and countesses
breakfasted at five in the morning on salt beef and herring,
a slice of bread, and a draught of ale from a black-jack.
Lords and servants dined in the same hall and shared the
same meal. As to dress, plain leather and woollen served
for all ranks, except on splendid ceremonials."

In this passage we have a patent mis-statement of the
case. It is certain that in a state approaching barbarism
there is but little difference in the general condition of the
headman of a tribe and an ordinary member of it—the
conditions of life are to each almost equally hard, and the
enjoyments of life almost equally limited. So in former
times there was little difference between the condition of the
earl and of the churl; both lived on a low level, so far as
the comforts and refinements of civilization were concerned.

A member of the middle class of society now has more
of the means that make life full and pleasant than the
noble of former days.   He has a more comfortable house,
better sanitary arrangements, better appliances in sickness,
less cruel methods of surgery; art, science, and literature
combine to make his life easy and elegant.   The products
of every country are to be found on his table: tea from
China, sugar from Barbadoes, salmon from Canada, pears
from California, grapes from Spain.   Every morning his
curiosity is gratified by the daily paper containing the
latest news, conveyed by telegraph or telephone from every
important city and country in the Old World and the New.

If he desires to travel, he can do so in a comfortable
railway carriage, secure of light and warmth, that will take
him rapidly to his destination, accomplishing in a day what
it would have taken more than a week, with weariness and
discomfort, to travel in what are sometimes called the good
old times.   If he wishes to cross the ocean to America, he
can do so in magnificent and well-appointed steamers,
having on board all the comforts of home, in a shorter time
than it used to take to come from England to Ireland,
the latter journey being now a less serious undertaking
than it used to be to go from London to Cornwall.

In all these modern improvements and advantages the
working classes have had their share.   Cheap books,
cheap and excellent daily and weekly papers, free libraries
where they can have access to the standard literature of
all ages, provide for their intellectual culture and enjoyment.   Cheap means of travelling, the tramcar the poor
man's carriage, the penny post, technical and general
education on easy terms, free or cheap access to museums

and picture galleries, the opportunity of hearing the music of the great masters well rendered at a merely nominal charge, make the condition of the working-man of the present day in many most important respects superior to that of the landed gentry of former times.

Dr. Giffen sums up the result of his very careful investigation by saying: " Thus the rich have become more numerous, but not richer individually; the poor are to some extent fewer; and those who remain 'poor' are, on the average, twice as well off as they were fifty years ago. The 'poor' have thus had almost all the benefit of the great material advance of the last fifty years."

An accurate observer of men and things in another land comes to the same conclusion. M. Anatole Leroy Beaulieu says: "Far from seeing their condition grow worse with the progress of industry, peasants and artisans are the two classes of society which have most benefited by the increase of wealth. Of the three factors of production, the three usual joint sharers in the products of industry, we find that labour is the one whose share tends to increase most rapidly. While interest upon capital and the profits of the employer have decreased with the progress of wealth, the workman's wages, the renumeration of labour, is ever increasing. The accumulation of capital tends to reduce its yield. This is a fact patent to the eyes of all who do not refuse to see it. The lazy egotism of the investors is justly complained of; each day it becomes more difficult to live upon the interest of one's investments. Even the rich, owing to the fall in the rate of interest, will soon find idleness inconvenient. We are witnessing a phenomenon which is nothing short of an economical revolution,—a revolution to the detriment of capital, and in favour of the proletariat."

We may now fairly assert that Mr. George's statement, that under the present system the rich are growing richer and the poor becoming poorer, is absolutely devoid of any foundation in fact, and expresses what is the exact reverse of the truth.

If we found that a physician had made a mistake in his diagnosis, we should not be disposed to trust the case any longer to his care. Yet it might happen that, mistaking the disease, he might also mistake the remedy, and the second mistake might so far correct his first error that his remedy might be the right one after all. It is an exceedingly unlikely supposition, yet it is a possible one. Mr. George has clearly misread the signs of the times, and does not see what is the exact condition and tendency of society; and we should be justified in refusing to consider the remedy he proposes for our social ills. Yet, like the physician, although his diagnosis has been incorrect, still he may possibly have stumbled on the true remedy. We shall examine the remedy he proposes.

We shall let Mr. George state it in his own words: "What I propose as the simple yet sovereign remedy which will raise wages, increase the earnings of capital, extirpate pauperism, abolish poverty, give remunerative employment to whoever wishes it, afford free scope to human powers, lessen crimes, elevate morals and taste and intelligence, purify government, and carry combination to yet nobler heights, is—to appropriate rent by taxation."

Mr. George has a quite exaggerated view of the evil of rent, and consequently an exaggerated view of the benefit

13

that would result from its abolition. In all his arguments like many Socialists, he carefully avoids inductive processes. His method is one by which it is difficult to arrive at a true, and easy to arrive at a false conclusion. At the same time, it is not so easy to detect the fallacy.

Regarding rent he says: "With the increase of productive power rent tends to even greater increase." "Rent swallows up the whole gain, and pauperism accompanies progress."

Let us see what abolition of rent would do for us. The condition of those lands in which there are no rents is not encouraging. In Russia there are no rents, yet the lot of the agricultural labourer is wretched in the extreme, and pauperism is greater in proportion, and more intense in its destitution, than in most countries in which rents are paid. In Norway there are no rents, yet in Norway there is a pauperism greater in proportion than in England.

Let us consider this question in connexion with England, a land in which rents are high and landlords flourish, and in which there are abuses, especially as regards ground rents, that are admitted on all hands. Yet Mr. George's statements break down even in England.

About two centuries ago, according to the statements of King and Davenant, which are by the best authorities regarded as trustworthy, the annual produce of England and Wales was forty-three millions, and the gross rental ten millions; that is, the rental was about twenty-three per cent of the produce. At present the produce of the United Kingdom is reckoned at twelve hundred millions, and the rental at seventy millions; that is, the rental is less than six per cent of the total produce. Rent falls from twenty-three to six per cent. Yet Mr. George tells us that, " with the increase of productive power, rent tends to greater increase "; and that " rent swallows up the whole gain, and pauperism accompanies progress."

Two centuries ago the average income of a working-class family was twelve pounds twelve shillings per annum ; the average income of a similar family now is eighty-one pounds. In numbers the working classes have increased six per cent, in income fourteen per cent; yet Mr. George says rent swallows up the whole gain. The facts are against him.

Now suppose that rent were to be abolished, what would it do for us ? Would it turn our darkness into light, and remove every social ill, as Mr. George says it would ? The local taxation of the country amounts to about seventy millions, the same figure as the rental of the country. Now can any one be so absolutely absurd as to believe that having local rates paid by the nationalization of the land would produce such marvellous effects as the abolition of ˙bad trade, insufficient wages, and pauperism ? Mr. George has no more skill in proposing a remedy than he had in discerning the disease. We might very fairly decline to consider any further his palpable fallacies, and would do so were it not that there is one which has so caught the popular ear that we must spend a little time in exposing and refuting it.

Mr. George tells us that there ought to be no private property in land for two reasons : first, because land is the gift of God ; and, second, because land is the gift of God to all, no one should monopolize what was intended for others

as well as for himself. He says the latest born London
street arab has as much right to the estates of the Duke
of Westminster as the duke himself. Consequently Mr.
George would divide the land with the street arab, and
that without any compensation to the duke—just as he
would take stolen property from a burglar without giving
him any compensation.

This scheme differs widely from that proposed by John
Stuart Mill. He would allow the landlord fair compensation for improvements effected by him, and only confiscate
the unearned increment ; that is, the increased value which
had come without any increased expenditure. Land, it is
said, is the gift of God. Is it any more the gift of God
than trees or cattle, than diamonds or coal, than nitrate
beds or guano fields, or the harvest of the sea?

Mr. George says we may rightly hold property in that
which has been produced by human labour. But what is
that ? Mr. George gives us, as an example, the pen with
which he wrote. But was not the matter of which the
pen was made the gift of God ? Man cannot create, he
can only mould and fashion materials already created to
his hand.

Exactly the same is it with land. The land God gives
is not more intended for all than are the other gifts of
Providence. It requires, just as they do, the application
of human labour to make it valuable. Land must be
drained, fenced, ploughed, manured, if it is to be of
service to mankind. A large landowner stated a short
time ago that he had spent sixty thousand pounds in improvements on his estate during the previous few years.
Thousands of acres have been reclaimed in England and

Scotland at a cost of from twenty to thirty pounds an acre; that expenditure is as truly manufacturing agricultural land as spinning and weaving are manufacturing calico out of cotton or linen out of flax. It would be just as sound reasoning to say no man can hold property in calico because cotton is the gift of God, or no man can hold property in linen because flax is the gift of God, as to say no man ought to hold property in land because land is the gift of God.

In the encyclical of Pope Leo XIII., *De Conditione Opificum*, the case is well stated : " That which is required for the preservation of life, and for life's well-being, is produced in great abundance by the earth, but not until man has brought it into cultivation and lavished upon it his care and skill. Now when man thus spends the industry of his mind and the strength of his body in procuring the fruits of nature, by that act he makes his own that portion of nature's field which he cultivates, that portion on which he leaves, as it were, the impress of his own personality ; and it cannot but be just that he should possess that portion as his own, and should have a right to keep it without molestation."

Mr. George's scheme of land nationalization, which is really a scheme of confiscation, we must therefore regard as being inadequate to do what he says it could accomplish, as being unjustifiable by any arguments adduced in its favour, as being injurious to society, because it would destroy that sense of confidence and security which is essential to commercial prosperity, and as being distinctly immoral because it violates the divine law.

CHAPTER XVI.

The Iron Law of Wages—What the Worker is entitled to—Right of
the Labourers to combine—Adam Smith—State Interference on
behalf of the Worker a principle of the English Economists and
not the result of the Socialist Movement—The Central Issue—
Marx's Fallacy—Advantages of Private Property—The Sacredness
of Property—The Encyclical *De Conditione Opificum*—Case of
Samoa—Failure of Socialist Communities—The Law of Interest—
The Law of Inheritance.

SOCIALISTS speak of the "iron law of wages" by which a
mere subsistence wage is all that can be obtained by the
labourer. They say that outside the margin of those
employed are the unemployed, who must be willing to
work for what will keep them alive, and that the unemployed competing for work with the employed will
always keep wages down to the lowest point that will
enable the worker to live. Thus they say that the present
system of free competition in production is in its very
nature and results cruelly unjust to the worker.

Christianity teaches us that " the labourer is worthy of
his hire," that he should receive "that which is just," and
that nothing due to him should be "kept back by fraud."
It condemns "grinding the faces of the poor," and everything that savours of oppression and spoliation.

On Christian principles the worker ought to get what
will enable him to obtain sufficient nourishment to keep
him in good health, suitable clothing, and a wholesome

and comfortable home. He ought not to be compelled to work so long as to prevent him from having time for recreation, for worship, and for mental and social enjoyment. If at all possible, these things should be secured to him. What may be called the Christian law of wages demands this.

Workers have a right to protect themselves by combination. It is impossible on any principle of natural justice to object to combinations, either of capitalists or labourers, for mutual protection. Trades unions are defensible, and it is only fair that their members should succour each other in any conflict that may arise between capital and labour. That trades unions should have the power of compelling all workers to belong to them is a clear interference with individual liberty. Trade combinations should be voluntary associations. Any who do not choose to join them should have the liberty of selling their labour on their own terms. Combination may be trusted to modify the evils of unlimited competition, and the amount of free labour outside of combinations will modify the evils that might result from the unreasonableness of combined labour.

Just as amongst nations, circumstances may arise that would justify war, so in trade disputes, circumstances may arise that would justify a strike or a lock out. In calmly looking back on the history of nations, we come to the conclusion that very few wars have been justified by their results. In the majority of cases the evil has overbalanced the good.

So as regards strikes. There has been a longer or a shorter struggle; bitter feelings have been aroused; much

suffering inflicted, especially on women, children, and old
people; and in most cases no permanent good has been
secured. The balance of advantage, both moral and material,
is against the " strike " as well as against the " lock out."
The wiser and the more fully imbued with the principles
of Christianity nations become, the less ready are they in
every quarrel to resort to the stern arbitrament of the
sword. So as wiser counsels prevail amongst working
men and capitalists, the more will they try to come to
terms without resorting to the last appeal—the strike or
the lock out.

Professor Thorold Rogers says: "The leaders and managers
of labour partnerships have very rarely formed a correct estimate of the powers at their disposal, and the powers which
they strive to resist and overcome, for the immediate object
of a strike has only occasionally been obtained. They who
combine for these ends have the mortification of knowing
and seeing that their sacrifices and labours in the machinery
of their organization are made by a small portion of the
order to which they belong, while the benefit of their
action, if it be successful, is shared by those who decline
to participate in the movement, and even take advantage
of the occasion to baffle those who assert, and with perfect
sincerity, that they are labouring for the common good
of all their fellows."

Arbitration affords a method by which trade disputes
might be settled to the general advantage and comfort of
the community, as well as for the mutual benefit of
capitalists and workmen. In the city of Dublin a Council
of Arbitration is in operation, some members of which
have been elected by the town council and some by the

associated trades; and this council has intervened several times in disputes with the happiest effect.

It is reported that encouraging results have attended the first year's working of the Conciliation Board set up by the London Chamber of Commerce. A number of disputes have been amicably settled, and in some cases the board has been instrumental in restoring employees to work which they had temporarily lost in consequence of trade disputes. At first the board started on the plan of only using its influence for peace where requested to do so. It has, however, found its efforts responded to so cordially and courteously by labour as well as by capital, that it is now able to develop its operations and boldly take the initiative by offering its mediation to both parties at an early stage of a trade dispute. Separate conciliation boards or committees are now being instituted for each trade. That for the boot and shoe trade is already in existence, and progress is being made with the establishment of similar boards for the textile, furnishing, musical instrument, engineering, printing, and allied trades, bargemen and lightermen, carmen, coal porters, and millers No less than sixty trades unions are now connected with the central board; they have accepted its principles by sending delegates to its meetings. The movement is also spreading throughout the country. Twenty-four conciliation boards have been established by chambers of commerce in the great towns of England.

Christianity does not settle the exact wages a man should receive, nor the number of hours he ought to work. It lays down certain principles, and on these principles men are to make the specific arrangements for themselves according to the circumstances of the age and country.

That gross injustice has been inflicted on workers cannot be denied. Before the passing of the factory acts, women and children worked beyond their strength, so that they were terribly injured, both physically and mentally. At present in Russia children work thirteen hours, as long as the men; and in Austria they are compelled to keep busy fifteen and even seventeen hours, exclusive of meals.

Socialists claim all the credit for modern legislation in favour of the worker, and say it is the result of their agitation; they also condemn the present system as inevitably leading to the exploitation of the worker, and therefore argue that the present *régime* should be overturned as speedily as possible. Neither the one assertion nor the other is correct.

Laisser faire has never been accepted as a principle by English economists. Mr. Herbert Spencer stands practically alone in his extreme individualism. He cannot be said to have founded a school. He has no following. He has simply presented, with great ability, his theory that the State has only one function—that of administering justice. He has signally failed to show why the State should not do for the individuals composing it that which promotes their welfare, and which they could not do or could not so well do for themselves.

Adam Smith, the founder of English political economy, who is often spoken of as being well-nigh as extreme an individualist as Mr. Herbert Spencer, yet lays down principles of which recent social legislation is the natural fruit. Advocating popular education, he says: " The same thing may be said of the gross ignorance and stupidity which in a civilized society seems so frequently to benumb the understanding of all the inferior ranks of people. A man without the proper use of the intellectual faculties of a man is, if possible, more contemptible than even a coward, and seems to be mutilated and deformed in a still more essential part of the character of human nature. Though the State was to derive no advantage from the instruction of the inferior ranks of people, it would still deserve its attention that they should not be altogether uninstructed."

He thinks that some sort of military training should be imparted to the people, and says: "To prevent that sort of mental mutilation, deformity, and wretchedness which cowardice necessarily involves in it from spreading themselves through the great body of the people, would deserve the serious attention of government, in the same manner as it would deserve its most serious attention to prevent a leprosy or any other loathsome and offensive disease, though neither mortal nor dangerous, from spreading itself among them, though perhaps no other public good might result from such attention besides the prevention of so great a public evil."

Smith also supported the suppression of the truck system, and maintained that its abolition was "quite just and equitable; that it did not improperly interfere with freedom of contract; that it imposed no real hardship on the masters; it only obliged them to pay that value in money which they pretended to pay, but did not really pay, in goods."

Thus Smith admits the propriety of the State, not

merely taking upon itself the duty of administering justice,
but also acting in the interests of the public in matters
affecting the health, the education, the convenience, and the
general wellbeing of society.

In accordance with these views are the declarations of
M'Culloch, one of Adam Smith's ablest and most illustrious
followers. He also speaks wisely and strongly on the
subject of the housing of the working classes.

"Such cottages," he says, "being cheap, are always sure
to find occupiers. Nothing, however, can be more obvious
than that it is the duty of government to take measures
for the prevention and repair of an abuse of this sort. Its
injurious influence is not confined to the occupiers of the
houses referred to, though if it were, that would be no
good reason for declining to introduce a better system.
But the diseases engendered in these unhealthy abodes
frequently extend their ravages through all classes of the
community, so that the best interests of the middle and
higher orders, as well as of the lowest, are involved in this
question. And, on the same principle that we adopt
measures to guard against the plague, we should endeavour
to secure ourselves against typhus, and against the brutalizing influence, over any considerable portion of the population, of a residence amid filth and disease."

Here it is admitted that the State has a right to inter-
vene to save its subjects from degrading and brutalizing
influences, that they should be saved from them when
those influences might result from the carelessness or
cupidity of others, and that they should even be prevented
from degrading themselves.

Hence we conclude that a great part of recent legislation

for the benefit of the working classes is not due to
Socialism, but is the natural working out of principles
long maintained by English economists, and would have
taken place had such a thing as Socialism never been
heard of.

We have to consider some of the theories propounded
in the standard work on the Socialist side of the economic
controversy, Marx's *Das Kapital*. The antichristian bias
of his mind is strikingly shown in this work. It might
have been thought that in a book dealing with financial
matters no attack would have been attempted on any
system of religion, but Marx could not let any opportunity
pass by him of expressing his contempt for Christianity.
In this evil work he is " instant in season and out of
season."

In discussing a simple equation of value he remarks :
" The fact that it is value is made manifest by its
equality with the coat, just as the sheep's nature of a
Christian is shown in his resemblance to the Lamb of
God." It is hard to say which is the more striking in
this illustration, its want of aptness or its want of reverence.
Without any necessity to refer to the religious question
at all, he says : " In order therefore to find an analogy,
we must have recourse to the mist-enveloped regions of
the religious world. In that world the productions of
the human brain appear as independent beings endowed
with life, and entering into relation both with one another
and with the human race. So it is in the world of
commodities with the products of men's hands."

These relations between commodities which exist in
the imagination of Marx, instead of being like the inde-

pendent beings of the religious world, are more like the
creations of an ill-balanced genius which are unsym-
metrical and inharmonious.   His theories do not account
for existent facts, and are not compatible with truths that
can be demonstrated with mathematical certainty.

The central issue in the whole socialistic controversy is
Marx's doctrine of surplus value.   Suppose, he says, the
working day to consist of twelve hours, during the first
six of which the worker confers as much value (say in
making boots out of leather) as would amount to his own
subsistence, the amount he actually receives; then during
the remaining six hours he works for his employer for
nothing.   This surplus value becomes the employer's
capital.   It should belong to the worker.   Labour is the
only source of wealth and the sole element in value.   In
order then that justice should be done, there ought to be
no private property, the means of production ought to be
held collectively, the products themselves kept by the
State, and divided amongst the workers in accordance with
the socially necessary time they have spent in the service
of society.

The fallacy of Marx is that he makes labour the only
source of value.   The Physiocrats traced up all capital
to land, and ignored the claims of labour.   The exactly
opposite mistake is made by Marx.   Labour will not create
value unless it is labour wisely expended on something
furnished to us by nature. Labour spent in " beating the
air " will not create value.   Hence, in considering value,
we must start with some natural product that can be
turned to good account by the expenditure of human
labour upon it: as labour spent on cotton in making

calico, that is useful for many purposes, as clothing, book-binding, etc.

But we must add to this labour, ability to conduct business, knowledge of materials and of markets, enterprise that will venture to make goods for which there is not immediate demand, and that will extend commerce by seeking for new customers, if necessary in new markets and probity that will secure the confidence of those with whom business is carried on.

To say that labour ought to get all the results of commerce, when it is only one element out of at least five which are engaged in the making of capital, is manifestly unfair. Thus the most important economic idea of Socialism is a great fallacy. If labour were the sole source of wealth, we should be logically and morally bound to accept all the parts of the socialistic scheme which properly follow from this supposition ; but as labour is not the sole source of wealth, Socialism in its economic aspect, resting mainly on this foundation, falls to pieces.

It is further evident that the labourers have no right to all capital, since it is not, as Marx calls it, " congealed labour," and that private property is not a standing grievance to all workers.

We have already seen that Christianity sanctions the principle of private property, and we shall now show that this principle is one which is very advantageous to society ; and thus have an additional proof that Christianity is in favour of the prosperity of society, and in accordance with sound political economy, whilst Socialism is antagonistic to both.

In the encyclical *De Conditione Opificum* it is said :

" Thus it is clear that the main tenet of Socialism, the
community of goods, must be utterly rejected; for it
would injure those whom it was intended to benefit, it
would be contrary to the natural rights of mankind, and it
would introduce confusion and disorder into the common-
wealth. Our first and most fundamental principle therefore, when we undertake to alleviate the condition of the
masses, must be the inviolability of private property."

Let us imagine, for the sake of argument, that society
is reconstituted on socialistic principles. Every man now
is sure of some, even if of a very insufficient supply of
his ordinary wants; but no one can become the owner of
private property, no one can save and hand down his
savings to his children. There is equality of condition.
The words of the socialist song, " We all shall equal be,"
have been realized. Taking human nature as we know it
to be, the majority of men, sure of their daily bread, would
do as little work as possible. To suppose otherwise is
to suppose that Socialism, without any adequate motive
or power, would make an immediate change in human
nature, so that men would at once cease to be egotistic
and become altruistic.

It is a universal experience that, leaving out those who
act from a sense of duty towards God, the overwhelming
majority act under the influence of a desire to promote
their own enjoyment. They take a near and narrow view.
Knowing the uncertainties of the future, as to continued
existence, opportunities of pleasure, and the faculty of
enjoyment, that may not only be destroyed by death,
but diminished by old age, accident, or sickness, they adopt
the old advice of Horace's *Carpe diem*, and seize eagerly

on present enjoyments, even at the expense of future well-being.

If the powerful motives presented by Christianity—motives drawn from an eternal future, from a personal Saviour and a personal God—in so many cases fails to prevent men acting thus, is it not absurd to suppose that Socialism would do so—especially when we consider the motives that Socialism can supply, and its teaching, that after this brief life the human being will cease to have individual consciousness or existence ; and that all who have died have " faded into the infinite azure of the past"? To suppose that Socialism would do what even Christianity in many cases has failed to do, is to suppose that an inadequate force can do what an adequate force rarely accomplishes—is to suppose that a train just moved by an engine of five hundred horse-power could be moved at an accelerated speed by the touch of an infant's finger.

It is thus certain that the majority would do their work perfunctorily,—even more so than they do at present ; and even the minority, who by their push and enterprise and invention promote the progress of society, would be disheartened. The stimulus that leads those men to work and think as they do is largely the desire to possess private property. This stimulus being withdrawn, the processes of production would soon suffer and become less efficient, and, as the result, the products of industry would deteriorate, both in quantity and in quality.

On the other hand, there would be an increase in the population. The difficulty of providing for families being taken away, families would be larger and more people would marry, so that a larger number of families would

14

be formed. Thus there would be a diminishing amount
for consumption, and an increasing number of consumers
—the necessary result being a less satisfactory portion for
each one. Society would be on the down grade, and
rapidly moving on to a much less civilized condition than
exists at present.

The history of the world confirms the truth of these
deductions. In all ages and nations economic progress
has been in proportion to the security of private property.
Capital is very sensitive, and where there is no security
there will be no accumulation of it; and where there is
no accumulation of capital, there can be no carrying on of
the processes of production on a large or progressive scale.
Thus destroying private property is really destroying
capital. It is killing the goose that lays the golden egg.
Socialism might introduce a state of universal poverty; it
cannot introduce one of universal wealth.

In most commercial states all this has been so deeply
and instinctively felt that the laws have been made unduly
favourable to the holders of property. Crimes against
property have been punished with an altogether dispropor-
tionate severity, as compared with crimes against the
person. A hungry man will be punished for stealing a
loaf of bread or a few turnips well-nigh as severely as
the drunkard who kicks his wife to death, and far more
severely than the drunken mother who oversleeps her child,
and awakes to find the infant dead. This very dispropor-
tion shows how deeply commercial nations have felt that
the sacredness of property must be enforced, or that their
prosperity must cease.

In those lands in which the sacredness of property is

not an accepted doctrine, there is no commercial prosperity, neither is there any advance in civilization. In Samoa, for example, a man may take anything he wants from his neighbour without paying for it. He may quarter himself in his neighbour's house, and make it his house as long as he likes. These customs originated in a well-meant desire to prevent destitution. They have, however, been the ruin of the island. Dr. Turner sums up his account of it by saying: " This communistic system is a sad hindrance to the industrious, and eats like a canker-worm at the roots of individual and national progress. In Brook Farm, in the United States, cultured and well-intentioned people tried Socialism on a small scale, and found it a failure. It is not adapted to human nature. Amongst those who joined in making the experiment was Horace Greeley. He sympathised with the earnest men who were in the community, but found in it those who prevented the success of the experiment—of scores of whom, he said, the world is quite worthy, the conceited, the crotchety, the selfish, the headstrong, the pugnacious, the unappreciated, the played out, the idle, the good for nothing generally, who, finding themselves utterly out of place and at a discount in the world as it is, rashly conclude that they are exactly fitted for the world as it ought to be."

Similar is the testimony of another member, W. H. Chauncey: " The great evil, the radical practical danger, seemed to be a willingness to do work half thorough, to rest in poor results, to be content amidst comparatively squalid conditions, and to form habits of indolence."

Owen's community at Yellow Springs failed, as one of its members stated, because " the industrious, the skilful, and the strong saw the products of their labour enjoyed by the indolent and the unskilled and the improvident, and self-love rose above benevolence. A band of musicians insisted that their brassy harmony was as necessary to the common happiness as bread and meat, and declined to enter the harvest field or the workshop. A lecturer upon natural science insisted upon talking only while others worked. Mechanics, whose day's labour brought two dollars into the common stock, insisted that they should in justice work only half as long as the agriculturist, whose day's work brought only one." The desire of private property is the stimulus that human nature needs in order that there may be a general advance in prosperity. The fear of poverty is a most important preventive of indolence. The principle of private property is one which is of the highest advantage to society, and its abolition, advocated by Socialism, would lead to social ruin.

Although the keenest attack of Socialism is directed against private property, it attacks, with only less persistency, two laws that are closely associated with it, and that are two great causes of our present inequality—the law of interest and the law of inheritance. The borrowing of money from banks and other institutions is not only a matter of great convenience, but a matter of absolute necessity to the carrying on of industry on a large scale. If men could not get interest they would not run the risk of lending; and not only so, but if they could not get interest they would not save to the extent that they do at present. Therefore abolishing the law of interest would tend to the diminution of business facilities, of the amount of private property, and consequently of the welfare of the community.

It is said that Christianity is opposed to the payment of interest. The Sermon on the Mount is quoted. "Give to him that asketh thee, and from him that would borrow of thee turn not thou away." Now this command simply inculcates a spirit of benevolence and of readiness to oblige and serve our fellows. It is not to be interpreted literally, any more than the command, "If thy right eye causeth thee to stumble, pluck it out, and cast it from thee."

A literal obedience to the command, "Give to him that asketh thee," would soon put one in such a position as to render compliance with the spirit of it impossible; for such a one would very soon have nothing to give, even if he started with the wealth of the Rothschilds. It cannot be correct interpretation of Scripture which would thus make its commands self-destructive.

In the parables of the talents and of the pounds it is implied that it is right to take "usury." We would not like to base a principle on a detail in a parable, were it not that Christ gives the lord who approves of taking usury as representing Himself. He would scarcely have done so if taking what is there called usury, although not used in the ordinary sense of the word—unlawful interest—were essentially wrong. Here again we find that Socialism does, and Christianity does not, condemn that which is of advantage to the permanence and progress of society.

It is an essential part of the socialistic scheme that the law of inheritance shall cease. We admit that the "power of the dead hand" ought to be modified. No man has a right to bind future generations to do that which is against their belief or their interests, hence the living may rightfully exercise a very great control over the testamentary dispositions of the dead. This power is being exercised more and more every year. The "death duties" may well be employed in lightening the burden of the living. That the more distant the relative to whom property is bequeathed the heavier should be the legacy duty, seems a very reasonable principle.

At the same time, we maintain that a man who has acquired property should be able to transmit it to his children, or to other persons whom he may select; or for certain definite purposes, as, for instance, the teaching of religion, or of science, or the relief of the poor and the sick. To determine that no man could have more than a life interest in any property that he might accumulate would cause a great depreciation in its value. This would be most unjust to the present holders.

It would also be injurious to society. It would be a direct incentive to extravagance. For a man, knowing that he could not leave his property in accordance with his wishes, would spend all he could during his lifetime. National thrift would decline. The capital of the country would be diminished. A wisely controlled right of bequest is undoubtedly for the interest of society. It is in accordance with the spirit of Christianity. "Parents should lay up for the children." Every man should provide for those of his own house, or else he "denies the faith," and is worse than an infidel. That surely includes providing for his family as far as he can, not only during his lifetime, but *after his decease?* How else can he do this except by the law of inheritance?

CHAPTER XVII.

Present Condition of Society unsatisfactory—Hopeful Tendencies in Society—Evils of Socialism—Impossibility of establishing Socialism—Sufficiency of Christianity.

THE facts and arguments that have been adduced, we submit, serve to establish the following propositions:

I. That the present condition of society is very far from being satisfactory, inasmuch as it suffers from many serious evils—such as ignorance, destitution, and gross forms of immorality—which might be, and ought to be, removed.

II. That whilst the condition of society is not satisfactory, it is not deteriorating, as Socialists tell us; nor yet is it, as they assert, so hopeless that nothing less than a revolution and a fresh reconstruction of society will avail to make life really a blessing, and an object of desire to its possessor.

III. That in society at present there are many hopeful tendencies, amongst which may be mentioned a tendency rather to the diffusion than to the concentration of capital; a tendency to increase the rate of wages, and to diminish the hours of labour; a tendency towards a more equitable division of the means of enjoyment; a tendency towards increasing sympathy amongst the different classes of society; and a tendency to increased respect for individual liberty.

IV. That if Socialism could be established, it would

make life excessively dull by reason of its uninteresting
uniformity, and would place the masses under a system of
tyranny and oppression that would soon become intolerable.

V. That if Socialism were established, it would be found
to be a system so untrue to the facts of human nature, that
by a natural and inevitable evolution society would free
itself from the incubus that would prevent the full play
of its forces.

VI. That the hope for society is not by going forward
to revolution or backward to superstition, not in the Red
International nor the Black, but in the gradual evolution
of society by enlightened and progressive legislation under
Christian influences.

VII. That to establish Socialism would probably be
found an impossible task.

Who would be against it? Not a few millionaires only,
but all the thrifty who had anything to lose, all men of
independent spirit who prized individual liberty as one of
the greatest of earthly blessings, all true patriots who do not
want to see their country dominated by the vilest, all who
believe in the providential government of God, and that
His past government has not been an unmitigated blunder,
so that now an entirely new method must be adopted.

Now when all these are on one side, and restless revolutionists, and utopian dreamers, and those who believe that
it would suit their purpose and capacities to fish in troubled
waters, are on the other, the issue is not doubtful. Take
Mr. Burns' illustration. The Socialists, he says, are the
wolves behind the sledge. They are many, and the driver
one; therefore they triumph. But if there had been as
many men on the sledge as there were wolves behind it,

and the men well armed and active, would the wolves triumph ?

Even so, if the State and the Christian elements in society put forth their strength, revolutionists will not succeed. It is to be regretted that so much energy and intellect have been given to the work of destruction, or to a vain striving after the unattainable. Far better would it have been for all if those valuable forces, instead of being wasted, had been spent in practical effort to improve the condition of society.

Socialism is unnecessary ; Christianity is sufficient for all our needs. Christianity tells us of a brotherhood of Christians, bound together in sympathy and love ; but it also presents to us the broader brotherhood of a common humanity. Now let this idea of brotherhood permeate our souls, and we shall not leave our fallen and degraded and in many cases personally offensive brethren alone. As we would not leave a brother according to the flesh alone because he was afflicted with some loathsome disease, so we shall not leave our morally diseased brethren alone to perish in their sins. We shall try to heal the moral leper. We shall try to raise the spiritually dead.

Let the principles of Christianity rule over the hearts and lives of men, and then oppression, and fraud, and overreaching, and squalid poverty, and foul slums, and sweating shops, and opium dens, and gambling hells, and the multiplied allurements to drunkenness, and unrighteous gains, and the envy of the poor towards the rich, and the pride of the rich scorning the poor, will cease. Let the principles of Christianity be operative in all those who profess and call themselves Christians, and instead of a selfish spirituality, or a putrescent cant, or a pompous formalism, such as we sometimes witness, let there be always and everywhere amongst Christians a true, enlarged, and enlightened spirituality, consisting of a sincere love to God and to man, a simple, honest following of the precepts of Christ, and soon our social difficulties will vanish, our bitter feuds will end, righteousness will exalt us, and we shall have " peace within our walls and prosperity within " not only our " palaces," but all our dwellings.

INDEX OF SUBJECTS AND PERSONS.

www.ingramcontent.com/pod-product-compliance
Lightning Source LLC
Chambersburg PA
CBHW030343270326
41926CB00009B/948